Terri Murphy's e-listing and e-selling secrets

For the Technologically "Clueless"

While a great deal of care has been taken to provide accurate and current information, the ideas, suggestions, general principles, and conclusions presented in this text are subject to local, state, and federal laws and regulations, court cases, and any revision of same. The reader is thus urged to consult legal counsel regarding any points of law–this publication should not be used as a substitute for competent legal advice.

Publisher: Diana Faulhaber
Senior Managing Editor: Ronald J. Liszkowski
Production Management: Omega Publishing
Art and Design Manager: Lucy Jenkins

© 2001, 1996 by Dearborn Financial Publishing, Inc.®

Published by Real Estate Education Company,®
a division of Dearborn Financial Publishing, Inc.®
155 North Wacker Drive
Chicago, IL 60606-1719
(312)836-4400
http://www.REcampus.com

All rights reserved. The text of this publication, or any part thereof, may not be reproduced in any manner whatsoever without written permission from the publisher.

Printed in the United States of America.

00 01 02 03 10 9 8 7 6 5 4 3 2 1

Library of Congress Cataloging-in-Publication Data

Murphy, Terri.
    Terri Murphy's e-listing & e-selling secrets for the technologically clueless/by Terri Murphy,–2nd ed.
      p. cm.
    Rev. ed. of: Terri Murphy's listing & selling secrets. c1996.
    Includes bibliographical references and index.
    ISBN 0-7931-3548-6
      1. Real estate listings–Computer networks. 2. Real estate business–Computer networks. 3. Real estate agents. 4. Internet marketing.
5. Internet advertising. I. Title: Terri Murphy's e-listing and e-selling secrets for the technologically clueless. II. Title: E-listing & e-selling secrets for the technologically clueless. III. Title: E-listing and e-selling secrets for the technologically clueless. IV. Murphy, Terri. Terri Murphy's listing & selling secrets. V. Title.
HD1382.6 .M87 2000
333.33'068'8–dc21

                                      00-023237

Acknowledgments

You know you're in trouble when you can't even begin to thank everyone who has put up with your whining, complaining, frustration, and kvetching when a project like a book fills your life. With that said, I very much want to extend my sincerest thanks to all of those special people who put up with me during the process of writing this book.

Richard L. Davidson, Ph.D. and master of "life balance," who was continually gentle and supportive (well, most of the time) as "we" swashbuckled through piles of papers and rewrites. Thank you especially for the brilliant ways you got me to enjoy a lunch break to make me all better, got me back on track when I went astray, and consistently pointed out my blessings when I lost my way—and yes . . . for the presents!

To my tech goddess, Web princess, and computer diva, Cherise Greski-Lesniewicz, for the last-minute double and triple checks on all things technological and for answering my panic calls as things disappeared, froze, crashed, and often burned. I especially appreciate her speaking real English as she helped me to refer to tech tools by their real names instead of "thingy's." ;-)

To my office staff—Yvonne Drewanz, Connie Catharine, Donna Sears, and Scott Flesch—and manager, Colleen Fleming, at the Coldwell Banker office for covering for me while I was buried in manuscripts. To Diana Faulhaber at Dearborn and Christine Litavsky for hanging in there during the trials and tribulations. To Edward DesRoches for my first writing opportunity, with more that followed in the years thereafter. Thanks for being such a close friend and respected colleague.

And, of course, a special thank you to the lady who taught me the real estate business to begin with . . . Ms. Penny Sirott. She helped me develop my confidence and taught me to understand the power of knowledge. By my standards, she's the best teacher in the business.

To all of you, my heartfelt and sincerest gratitude and love for helping me to help others. Grazie, Grazie, Grazie!

Contents

Preface   vii

1. e-Listing & e-Selling with 21st Century Technology   1
2. The New e-Consumer, e-Shopping, and e-Service   15
3. Connecting with Digital Communication   27
4. The Building Blocks of Your Electronic Presence   49
5. Designing Your Web Presence   71
6. Farming with 21st Century Communication Tools   95
7. Selling *You* Before the Listing Appointment   109
   Prelisting Package   131
8. An e-Look for Your Next Listing Presentation   157
9. Cool Stuff You Should Know   167
10. e-Prosper & Live Longer: Life Balance and 21st Century Real Estate   177

Appendix A: Backing Up Data   199
Appendix B: Sample e-Newsletters   205
Index   227
About the Author   235

Preface

This won't be the most technologically sophisticated book you'll ever read. It's not meant to be. I wrote this guide for agents like myself who need some kind of guidance through the initial phases of learning how to understand the Internet as it applies to our new roles in listing and selling real estate.

This book is written for the person who is confused and intimidated by the computer itself; for those who are frustrated trying to figure out what to buy, at what price; for those who don't even know what questions to ask; and for those who feel maniacal because of the attention and training required to get in the swing of things.

It took me about 2 1/2 years to learn about the Internet and actually use a computer; two plus years before I could incorporate the World Wide Web and e-mail for both marketing and making money listing and selling or developing "e-commerce."

For the person who doesn't have a clue, the entrance to the Internet world can be a bit overwhelming. With investments of time and money—for hardware, software, Web sites, tech tools, and training—this is no place to make a mistake.

Are you getting a gazillion calls a day from people trying to "sell" you their "full technology package"? There is a ton of confusing information from lots of people, all wanting to sell their "solutions" to our dilemma. Unfortunately, in many cases we don't even know if what they are selling is what we actually need, since we have not yet been able to establish a value set or a marketing strategy for our own Internet promotion.

It's sad to see well-meaning agents spending lots of money for a tech person or company to "get them on the Web" with no plan or knowledge whether what they are getting will work for them and their business. There are certain basics that need to be followed. They are simple; you should be the center of your Internet promotion, and you should build your marketing presence around that center . . . *you!*

This book is not intended to be a software-training guide. Although there are suggestions throughout to help you apply a software application, they are there to accomplish an end result: to help you understand this new communication tool, to help you become more organized, and to help you to make more money.

This Internet thing really took me by surprise. I was going along smugly listing and selling a lot of properties, and then everything began to change. I can only imagine what the vinyl record makers felt when their world began to shift to cassettes and then to compact discs. I was pretty concerned. I had been listing and selling for over 21 years and suddenly I wasn't even sure if I would have a job by the end of the year. Who would have ever thought that MLS information would be accessible to *regular* people?

You and I have knowledge and valuable experience that give us a priceless insight and storehouse of information that can create special services. Consumers will pay for these services because they will save them the one commodity no one can buy: time. Saving time can reduce "stress," and the 21st century doesn't seem to be any less stressful!

The word is that the major companies are moving toward putting the entire real estate transaction process online. Part of this process will include responsibility "defaults" to complete tasks within the service mode. As the standardization of the industry continues to evolve, the online transaction will report how well we, as agents, service each transaction, as well as everyone else involved. Your rating as an agent will shift from strong production volume being a desirable trait, to the assignment of high value to the quality of your services. This centralized rating system will measure your results in service performance; a new measure of super agent. The consumer will now know if you are actually doing your job, especially if your cumulative scores are maintained over 10 to 12 past transactions. Imagine that . . . and you thought you were beyond report cards! The new key is how pleased your clients and customers are with your full spectrum of services.

Online, Web-based software will track and score the service end of our business with the lower players flunking out. The empowered consumer will be using their power to "get the best" and to drive down pricing while developing new criteria to select agents or companies. The "mystery" of the transaction is now revealed. With the online transaction, every facet of the transaction is trackable and definable and the consumer will understand who isn't doing the job, as will every other party to the transaction.

The consumer may choose to negotiate each and every service instead of just accepting the agent's recommendation for services. The consumer may be offered an array of options for services attached to a transaction, such as inspections, warranty companies, title services, or survey services. Web technology and e-mail communication can provide a menu of services in a timely fashion.

Waiting to become electronically adept, for the hardware to become cheaper, or for the software to become easier to understand, is a deadly game. Although the technology and software may get easier, the window of opportunity gets smaller and you get farther and farther behind the curve. The only way to provide top-level services is through automation and *systems* that work even when you aren't on site, and without your immediate intervention. The secret: *systems are the key to service* in this 21st century arena. Without them, don't even think you can compete.

Doing business without an electronic presence will be like trying to do business via a disconnected telephone. You need to be connected electronically to be in the game, *and* with a distinctive presence. With the industry moving online, you simply won't be considered accessible without being digital. The longer you fight it, the more opportunities you will miss.

But whenever there is a shift, new opportunity is born. There is no demand for the wringer washing machine these days because a better model has replaced it. People still need to wash their clothes and can now do so more easily and in a more time-saving way. A silly analogy perhaps, but true. We need to become a better model of agent.

Our role as a service provider needs to be expanded and developed far past any type of "full service" we've rendered before. The payoff will be in the added services *beyond* the house sale. We are the masters of ancillary services. It's a little like new home construction; we can make more money selling the upgrades than on the house itself. Therein lies our advantage. We've been recommending services for no direct compensation for years. We have the knowledge . . . it's time to use it. As John Tuccillo so brilliantly says in his book *The Eight New Rules of Real Estate*, "Information is free, but knowledge is priceless." Your new role is to become an information center.

Here's where the smart agent can win in the new game. We've got databases of information on clients, customers, local services, etc. This information is *priceless* when it is organized in a fashion useful in other marketing applications.

For the past 50 years we thought we sold houses, and we were pretty much hit or miss on the services that followed the sale. Some services were the responsibility of the attorneys or escrow departments. Others could be dealt with by the buyers or sellers themselves. We had no stake in those services and let many opportunities to offer extended services slip away.

Prior to the Internet, if you wanted housing information, you needed a real estate agent. Today's consumer doesn't need us to find a home; they can get all the information they want before they need the agent to "finish the job."

The world of real estate has always been about service, and, quite frankly, we had a lot of room to improve. The process was never quantified and never rated for satisfaction. Several of the major franchises and concerned smaller companies did their surveys but, in general, individual agents did little to improve on the last transaction or to be concerned about the customer's experience during the transaction.

Jeremy Conaway, visionary and consultant, comments that "we are no longer being paid as hunters." Since consumers don't need us to "find" the property necessarily, they will be looking for a menu of services to handle the ancillary items that accompany buying a property and starting life in a new place with new needs.

The emphasis has shifted from *property and information* to *exchange of information and continued services.* We are now finding our value as the "information brokers" of the new real estate generation.

So, quit kicking and whining about how tough it is and see if what I have to say here can help you out. If you really want to learn more about computers, think about a Windows class or Michael Russer's "e-POWER" course; both will give you a great kick-start. My goal is to have you ask the right questions, to get you what you want and need to be a vital and successful professional agent serving the public today . . . and to be e-powered!

—Terri Murphy with Jeremy Conaway

Chapter 1

e-Listing & e-Selling with 21st Century Technology

After 21 years of selling real estate, it comes to this . . . no more private MLS . . . no more proprietary information! Things changing constantly, mergers, new services, new networks.

Previously, finding homes for people was information only I as an agent could access, which made me very necessary to a client and customer. Now this once very proprietary information is accessible by anyone with a computer . . . at any time . . . from any place.

The Internet. All the information anyone could ever dream of, magically available with a phone call, delivered within seconds, in the comfort of his or her own home or office, without moving more than a few muscles. I was worried about my career. Why would a buyer or seller need me anymore?

A New Real Estate Customer

This new medium of communication now changes the game. Previously, we were highly paid, skilled hunters, compensated for seeking out the perfect home for our customer, or marketing their home through a private pool of inventory and information. Ahh . . . how things have changed. As the hunt is no longer an issue, our value for providing those services also changes. Real service, with all its many components, will define the "edge."

Today, the customer is more informed and has access to all kinds of information, including housing. Buyers arrive at our offices clutching a fistful of color printouts of properties they've "viewed" through major electronic portals of housing information. They've "walked" through these homes via a virtual tour, checked out the neighborhood demographics, and even have a printed map to get to the home. The client/customer now does the "hunting" before even meeting you. What is your new role? How do you stay relevant to the transaction? What is your next step? How do you become the "new" agent?

A New Real Estate Industry

Our whole industry is up for grabs. The Internet, e-commerce, surprising mergers, acquisitions, etc., have all impacted the "old" way of doing business. Simply, there will be no "old" way in real estate . . . it is forever changed.

I have been "blessed" (or "burdened") with learning the new technology before many agents even knew about it. I was the one who thought Internets, Intranets, and Extranets were three different holds of hairspray! I wasn't thrilled about this new "trend" or "fad" either, until I met with several very important technology coaches who have guided me every step of the way. Understand that I learned, but not without massive amounts of kicking, screaming, whining, and complaining about how well I had done for the past 21 years; I was a top producer for most of those years without this new fangled Internet thing.

Little did I know what a gift I had been given. Here I am now, in a unique position to help you get on the information highway from the perspective of a peer. I've learned how to apply these new technologies and communication tools to what we have done as agents for years. I've learned to combine these tools with new services. I can share a few ideas about how to navigate the road to becoming the savvy agent you will need to become to stay in the game.

Whether we like it or not, the Internet is here to stay. It has drastically changed the old ways of how we handled our listing and selling business. The good news is that for those of us who approach our careers as a business and not a hobby, choosing to take on this new application to our industry, we will be fortunate enough to *win* at the listing and selling game, not just compete.

You have often heard that real estate agents will be replaced by the Internet. There are plenty of people saying lots of things that may or may not turn out to be totally true. Not being up on the latest information and communication will keep *anybody* doing business in the new millennium out of the loop.

There are also a lot of people out there telling us what to buy to "survive" in the 21st century arena, but few telling us what to do with this stuff after we pay for it, or what makes it important or relevant to our business.

A New Beginning

If you've made the decision to make real estate your career, or if you are looking for the way to stay in the business, here's a survival checklist to follow. It will get you the new digital edge you need to travel the information highway.

Step #1: Find a Mentor with 21st Century Savvy

A fantastic way to learn about the real estate business is to begin as a buyer assistant for a busy automated top producer in your office, or spend the money to "monitor" that person for a day or so. When selecting a mentor, don't just look for the big numbers in volume. Check out the organizational abilities behind those big numbers. Lots of agents continue to do big business the old way, but alas, show little or no profit from their time investment. In the past we were impressed with those agents who racked up gigantic volume and enjoyed hundreds of transactions a year.

The new value-set parameter will be the ratio of customer satisfaction for services rendered on each transaction. What if you got a report card after each transaction from your client or customer? And what if that information became available to other consumers who were interested in securing an agent to work with? And suppose that information was available to anyone who wanted it through the World Wide Web? How do you think you would rate?

The agent with the highest service ratios is more likely to get the job than the agent grinding out the transaction numbers but with low ratings on customer service. In addition, many agents are generating huge dollars and cash flow, but in the final accounting they are keeping only a fractional amount of that cash flow as actual profit.

So, if you are checking out a success model, here are a few important things to watch for:

- Seek out the top producing agent who is committed to learning and doing the best job for today's market and who wants to embrace the new changes and communication tools addressing our business today. Find one with an impressive digital strategy and Web site that have proven to generate commission dollars.
- Take note of the hardware and software systems this agent is using. Find out what contact database is the preferred choice. Investigate what electronic communications are being used. What traditional types of direct mail, newsletters, etc., have been found to be *productive* and *profitable*?
- Pay to "shadow" a top producer for a half or a full day. Different top producing agents charge different fees, but they

are worth it. The information is out there for you to check out on your own. Seeing firsthand what has been working for a productive office saves you time, energy, frustration, and money!

- Find out if a top agent is interested in teaming up with you as a buyer assistant. A top producer gives you lots of opportunity to develop hands-on experience, while working under the guidance and reputation of a seasoned agent. Taking that agent's buyers out to show properties affords you a steady stream of customers without the hassle of generating new business and handling the paperwork. This arrangement will differ with each agent, but there are sales agents who cannot handle all the buyer leads they receive and are only too happy to turn over the showing part to an enthusiastic "let me at 'em" new person. Compensation varies as well. Some agents offer percentages, while others have bonus arrangements. Ask around and see if this type of system works for you. Implement the arrangement with a hard copy agreement letter to avoid misunderstandings about compensation should the situation change in the future.

- If you are new, look for an opportunity to be a licensed personal assistant to a top producer. Many top producers have personally trained several people who started out doing the clerical and marketing duties to assist them. There are several successful top producers who will hire you knowing that the position is one of training and will last about one year. After that time, you might consider working as a buyer assistant agent for this top producer and eventually develop your own circle of business. Where there is a will, there is a way . . . that is uniquely right for you!

Step #2: Interview a Successful Agent

Top producers are very busy. You need to know they quite clearly understand that their time is money. If you are asking for their time and shortcuts, it must be an equitable proposition for you both. If there is someone you admire, ask for an appointment. Ask what it would cost to do so. Most top producers can buy their own lunch or dinner; however, they might be flattered that you offer to pay for their time and expertise.

Your first tactic is to study your local market and interview those agents who seem to have a great system. For additional sources of information outside of your local competing area, check out new Web sites offering monthly memberships and training online. Sites like *iSucceed™.com* offer information and training for every level agent with 24-hour access for a monthly membership fee. These types of sites can offer you access to winning and successful ideas and are a great way to "keep connected" to the onslaught of innovative ideas and success systems globally. It is worth the fee to have streamlined information coming right to you on demand, to keep you in the know with what is new and useful.

Other traditional sources have been Star Power© tapes and materials through Howard Brinton, Allen Hainge Seminars© and Newsletters, and many, many more.

Regardless of how you secure the information, you need to design your business and to ask the right questions *for you*. Traditionally, good questions to ask a successful agent have included the following:

- How much income/volume did you make your first year? Last year?
- How did you handle family obligations?
- Did you provide for your tax obligations?
- What was your formula for calculating tax obligations?
- Did you get/have special disability insurance?
- When did you hire a part-time assistant?
- How do you pay the people who help you?
- What duties in your home and business did you find necessary to delegate?
- What was your biggest challenge?

Questions to ask the 21st century savvy agent might include the following:

- Do you use agent productivity software to organize your database and tracking?
- Do you use Quicken© or other financial software to track expenses for tax purposes?
- Have you found a personal productivity software package that handles your calendar, address book, contact database, and tasks? If so, which one do you prefer?
- Do you have your own Web site and to whom is it linked or framed?
- Did you develop guidelines for your Web site design?
- Do you have trackable evidence that your Web site makes you money?
- Do you have tracking on your Web site to help determine the source of your business?
- How do you track which marketing tools and services are working the best for you?
- How many of your clients and customers communicate with you via e-mail?
- Do you own your own Internet domain?
- Do you know your percentage of profit from your various marketing efforts?
- What new tools are you using to meet the 21st century requirements for continued and distinctive services?

Getting the answers to some of these questions will help you write your own business plan for your career. Knowing the answers, or designing your plan to fulfill the needs here, spells success and profit for your precious time and efforts.

Step #3: Begin by Treating Your Business Like a Real Business

Start building your business like a business! Look at your costs to begin or continue in the industry. Besides the necessary licenses, continuing education, and seminars, you need to look at a budget that can include the new tools you will need to stay in the game.

This means getting yourself into the technology mode isn't a choice anymore. It is, and will continue to be, the way information and communication are organized and exchanged. Take the time to plan out the tools and expenses you will need to practice in the new millennium. Years ago we needed a desk and a phone. Now we need more tools and services. Begin figuring the following into your current budget:

- Getting online with an Internet Service Provider (ISP)
- Registering and owning your own domain to secure a permanent e-mail address
- Securing/building a personal Web site
- Choosing an annual hosting service
- Purchasing hardware (laptop/desktop computer; cellular phone; pager; scanner; printer; digital camera; Palm Pilot)
- Acquiring software (agent productivity software; financial software; personal productivity software)
- Using additional marketing tools (such as sign riders with your Web and e-mail addresses to add to your yard sign information)

These are just a few of the basics you might need. Every second there is a new way/tool/gizmo for you to consider. *Just begin,* master the basics, and get going. Upgrading is relatively easy when you are already familiar with the use of these new tools.

Step #4: Begin by Keeping Good Records

One of the biggest mistakes a salesperson makes is not understanding the status of being an independent contractor, and the importance of good records, for both taxes and a good exit strategy. Yes, at some point your client database can make you money! As Michael Gerber, author of *The E-Myth* and *The E-Myth*

Revisited, says so well: "The biggest challenge any small business entrepreneur has while building a business is not working *in* your business, but *on* your business."

A fresh beginning in the recordkeeping department can make life so much more pleasant. The challenge is to learn how to run your new business like a real business from the very beginning. If you do it right every day, you won't have the nightmare of recreating records for April 15th. With the latest software programs available, keeping good records is easy and efficient. Use software programs to control and study expenses and income on a regular basis. Panicking around tax time with a pile of receipts and inconsistent records is not only stressful, it's counterproductive.

*T*ech *T*ip

Don't waste your productive time on a task that is easily and affordably done with a good software program.

A good program like Quicken© or QuickBooks© will allow you to enter each of your checks in a simple format so you can keep track of your expenditures and your deposits every month. How much more decisive could you be about investing in a new promotion if you knew the funds were available and in your budget to do so?

At the end of each month, with the push of a button, you can see what you have earned and what you have spent. It is imperative that you understand the "profit" part of your business to determine in an instant if/when to consider new programs, tools, and investments that come your way.

We all know the focus to make money in the real estate business relies on four basic things: list, sell, negotiate, and prospect. Bookkeeping is not one of these four moneymakers, but it is very important to the foundation of the business. Help those that help you by organizing your expenses and income from the get-go and begin using financial software that will empower you to track your income and expenses for future goal planning and strategies.

Step #5: Create a Digital Database

Keeping an updated database is imperative. You will need to electronically organize your client and customer base for several reasons. Updating information should be done with a software program that easily integrates with Internet applications.

One of the best ways to utilize the power of your database is to couple it with the use of mail list/list serv software to make keeping in touch easy. Many ISPs offer mail list software for around $150 to $300. The best use of a database is to use it to send information. Use a software program that you are comfortable using, such as ACT, TopProducer, Agent2000, or Goldmine, just to name a few. Whatever software you are using, choose one that is compatible with Web applications for broader exposure and easier dissemination.

A second reason to build a strong database is, of course, to have good records for quantifying your own business. Another reason is for the possibility of sharing or selling your database in the future, should you decide to partner, move out of an area, or "sell" your business.

Tech Tip

The 21st century model for e-commerce is information and your ability to use that information in multiple service applications.

Don't minimize your database information with haphazard files and archaic 3 x 5 cards. Get with the program and get digital!

Step #6: Get a Tech Coach

The psychiatrist of the 1970s and 1980s is being replaced by the need for a technology coach. Remember that our prime activities must be listing, selling, negotiating, and prospecting. So becoming a certified geek is not necessary, but we must consider the importance of understanding the new communication and the "appliances" that go with it.

Even if you are a top producing agent, don't be held hostage or pay way too much money for digital goods and services. It takes a small investment of time but you need to be in control of this new medium.

Real estate is one entrepreneurial business that saves you from investing in warehousing, storing, inventorying, and outright purchasing of products to sell. The new 21st century agent needs some extras to compete and survive. Guidance and on-going technology training and assistance shorten the curve to you becoming sophisticated about the use of the World Wide Web.

Step #7: Invest in Hardware and Software

With your tech coach, decide what hardware and software you can afford now and when you can expect to afford the "extras." Don't be caught with a carload of expensive tech tools you don't know how to use and that seem to be aging as you take them off the shelf. Buy what you can use, master it, and move on to the next. There is no reason to spend money on technology toys and tools unless you plan to learn how to use them and then do it! Studies have shown that many of us spend lots of money for new technology and have no follow-up plan to implement its many uses.

You will want to get digital to keep a competitive edge on the changes, your market, and your competition. New Web sites and technology tools are evolving and changing as you breathe, so if you are serious, a laptop computer is a must. The agent of today is "virtual" and not tied to the limitations of an office or a desk. Although a desktop computer is less expensive, it is not as versatile or mobile to fulfill the needs of real estate business as it is being conducted today.

A laptop loaded with a digital listing presentation will likely replace your flip chart and presentation book. Unlike printed collateral, which is often out of date as soon as the ink dries, a digital presentation can be updated in seconds and personalized with just a few keystrokes. For more information, see Chapter 8 for the full scoop.

The equipment and the programs change daily, but keep in mind, if you are a "newbie" to technology and real estate, you won't be as quick to change to the high-end hardware. Have your tech coach advise you on a minimum and maximum for hardware and software requirements.

Step #8: Get Training

Take a course in Windows and learn how to use presentation software to get you up and going. Windows is the basis for most everything, so one course can set you right up. Don't miss out on a good PowerPoint training course as well for strong and powerful listing presentations. The investment of a few hours will set you light-years ahead of the pack. Check out Chapter 9's "Cool Stuff You Should Know" with important links for information on training and education online!

Step #9: Develop a Business Plan

The new real estate agent realizes that just "playing" at real estate won't pay the bills or build financial freedom. The "young lions" of today and smart long-time agents know that they must work out a plan, and then work the plan to make the most of their time, energy, and investment.

Michael Gerber's books *The E-Myth* and *The E-Myth Revisited* outline many of the facets of a workable/working business plan for the small business entrepreneur. You must know where you want to go to get there; detailing the amount of time, money, and your "life" time that you plan to invest makes good sense.

With the hundreds of programs, consultants, tapes, etc., available, make it a priority to invest your attention and energy into getting a plan in writing for the entire calendar year. Work in checkpoints on a monthly and quarterly basis to determine if your strategies should change, adapt, abort, or seek new avenues. Failure is continuing to do the same things and expecting different results. Learning is the benefit of each "failure."

Things to cover in your business plan include the following:

- A review of the previous year
- Specific costs (include dues, license renewals, CE costs, etc.)
- Written goals for volume, production, and income
- Action plans for marketing, including direct mail, electronic mailings, printed collateral
- Categories for retirement, taxes, new equipment and tools, the "Murphy's Law" factor (unwanted surprises), etc.

There's more about building your business plan in Chapter 10 on life balance. It's important when planning a "life" strategy to include all phases. This is the rest of your life . . . every day, spent minute-by-minute . . . make it count!

Tech Tip

Get help, pay for it, and contact a mentor/manager/good business person to help keep you focused. Check your financial reports frequently and on a regular basis.

In the real estate industry it is somewhat difficult to predict just how the changes will affect us in many areas. With new expectations and a very different type of consumer, experience doesn't count as much as it used to, and former production levels are immaterial; it's a brand new game.

Always there are the survivors, those who choose to work outside of their comfort zones. They are not the whiners and complainers. This special group of people finds the opportunity in the "tragedy" and makes lemonade out of lemons. Keep your eye on these people . . . they've got the right attitude. No fear . . . look for the opportunity.

Chapter 2

The New e-Consumer, e-Shopping, and e-Service

There is always power in knowledge. For the beginner, there is an unmistakable confidence that comes with understanding the products and services available in the marketplace. To become "valuable" to any relationship, there are some basics that you as a rookie or seasoned (but not yet technical) agent will need to develop. Step one requires some due diligence, which means you need to devote time and energy to getting familiar with the new electronic terrain.

What Is the Web Anyway?

The World Wide Web is the area of the Internet where there is visual interaction of pictures, graphics, and text. These are accessed through an Internet address, called a URL (Universal Resource Locator). Simply put, it is the side of the Web where the actual Web sites and pages are viewed and accessed. Chapter 4 is devoted to communication on the Internet through e-mail. In this chapter we offer suggestions and ideas on how to better understand the extensive new ways that marketing and information can be disseminated on the Web.

Web sites are the part of the Internet that host our online businesses and our virtual worldwide offices. At this writing, there are many types of Web sites for you to choose from. The most basic site offers the simplest page featuring static information, often referred to as a *résumé page*. Other sites offer linking and are refreshed with new and continually updated information; thus offering up-to-the-minute content. The latest Web site tools can be incorporated into the design of your site with communication tools that provide informational reports and services 24 hours a day, automatically.

The newest type of Web site is called a *portal*, synonymous with a *gateway*. These sites are used as major starting points for individuals when they access the Internet. Examples of portals are Netscape, ZDNet (computers), and Inman (real estate).

Imagine the ability to put showing feedback comments on the Web, allowing your clients to access information on the status and progress of their transaction, advertising updates, marketing reports, and other content that would be important to them via the services you offer.

Currently there are companies that offer to feature the full process of the sales transaction, interfaced with all service providers and parties to the sale. This unveiling of the online transaction is the initial step to streamlining each transaction and making the status available to all involved.

This new way of reporting and providing information puts the entire process and progress of a transaction online, taking the mystery out of the real estate transaction. Status on each phase of the transaction will be available at any time by anyone that is involved; thus accountability and "true" service evolve to a new standard of practice. With all parties being online, it will be imperative for the agent to be proficient and comfortable with using the online medium This move toward standardization of the real estate transaction will push our agent service standards to be more rigorous with new accountability. The mega numbers of transactions completed by a single agent may not be as important as the agent's overall service ratings.

New Challenges for Service

Today's marketplace has changed drastically with the introduction of the Internet and the newest opportunities of how and where information is available. In almost every minute of every day, new Web sites are being offered to empower anyone (including buyers and sellers) to become aware of properties available to be bought and sold.

In the old days, the agent had the exclusive scoop through multiple listing services as to what inventory was offered for sale. This paradigm has shifted sharply with the introduction of the Internet and home inventory sites like *Realtor.com™*, *HomeSeekers™*, and *HomeAdvisor™*, where the public has access to what was once proprietary information. At this writing, anyone interested in buying or selling now has access to information by simply going online.

The Consumer Drives the Industry

The consumer of today has many more avenues for doing business on the Internet, including home buying or selling. Daily, more and more Web sites offer discounted services for almost anything, including home buying and selling.

The Internet offers free services that "train" the consumer to demand and expect more. Look at Blue Mountain Greeting Cards. You can send a gazillion electronic greeting cards, personalized right down to the music and the message, without cost. You can find Web sites offering free Windows courses right online. If you want decorating hints, you have myriad sites offering free "buy it to try it" services. How do they survive? Look at the ancillary services that are offered. Send Blue Mountain's greeting card and they offer you a link to send chocolates or flowers while you are at it. Everyone has to win at the e-commerce game, so begin to identify what additional types of services you can offer that go beyond the scope of your present listing and selling assistance.

Here's a thought: Our industry can no longer support the costs of doing business as we have in the past. New demands for improved service and information systems have put a huge financial burden on management, offices, and associations. Agent training has changed drastically since the early days; replaced with a much more vigorous course that includes technology training and more sophisticated (and expensive) equipment. Broker profits are a fraction of yesteryear. The consumer is being trained to get more competitive real estate services and information for "free." Ancillary services such as title, inspections, contractor repairs, and discounts are now being offered from outside the real estate industry to the consumer with or without the agent. These ancillary service providers compete for the service opportunities that used to come solely with buying and selling properties.

It is unthinkable isn't it? That our income would be so vastly changed just because the dynamics have changed? The digital online transaction is literally right around the corner. The reconstruction of our changed role affects our compensation as well. The "mystery" of the real estate transaction is now open information to all involved. The industry is growing toward a "standardization," as other industries have evolved in the past.

Unlike the old days, everyone who is a party to a contract will have access to the process, and the accessibility of that information will drive the service to a new and demanding level. Consolidation will be the name of the game for services. For us to be effective and relevant, we must fully understand the needs and wants of the new consumer. These consumer wants and needs include immediacy, ease of use, and multiple options.

IMMEDIACY

Consumers want it now . . . when "they" want it. No longer is information and service relegated to fixed business hours or holidays, wasting time on hold, or having to leave home to see a product and get information about its design or construction.

We don't need gas station attendants to get fuel, or salespeople to buy books, or personal assistance in purchasing hundreds of other services. The real estate industry is not much different. Consumers won't need agents for the same types of service they are now providing nor will they be limited by agent access or agent knowledge.

EASE OF USE

Today's consumer wants a "now" response to their requests and service requirements. We need to design our services with a fuller and continued application that extends beyond the basic services of a real estate transaction, equipped with an instantaneous function. Think of McDonalds. Will you wait 30 minutes for a Big Mac? Probably not. You have been conditioned to expect the quickness of the service and the predictability of the product for a specific price. Otherwise, you would be parking at a restaurant, sitting down, and waiting a minimum of 15 to 20 minutes for a similar meal for a much more expensive price. What's the difference? The delivery and the expectations. Quick is the name of the game, and the old model won't make it for today's demanding consumer.

OPTIONS

The buyer and seller of today are interested in knowing the alternatives for selecting goods and services. There are hundreds of Web sites offering goods and services. Consumers can develop a new educated "value-set" of criteria to select which of the many products and/or services offered suits them for a price and service level that meets their needs.

When faced with wanting the services of a real estate professional, a brand new offering is available for the homeowner to use. Instead of a neighbor referral or a walk through the Yellow Pages, a buyer or seller can go online and get all the information he or she needs to help in the selection of an agent.

A New Way of Selecting an Agent

HomeGain.com is a Web site designed for the homeowner to find an agent to sell a home. This is a BRAND NEW WAY to interview for prospective real estate services. Imagine, all of your professional information would need to be accessible for a prospective homeowner to determine if you are the agent to handle their real estate transaction. Are you ready for the new search criteria? Do you have an online marketing strategy? Do you have a full informational résumé to help "sell" you? Are you armed with recent testimonials from previous clients and customers that validate satisfactory customer service? Can you offer valuable information services and expertise that are automatically delivered to the consumer upon request, thus providing extended value and customer care?

These are just a few of the selection criteria the new consumers will be aware of when looking for an agent to represent them. If you don't have a digital profile, you'll be locked out of even competing for the job interview. If you aren't registered with HomeGain, think about the leads you could be missing. You could be enjoying this "matching service" as a passive way to prospect and get more leads. (See Chapter 7 for more info!)

Benefits You Can Provide

Everybody likes to get more than what they've paid for, and additional services or conveniences are important to today's consumer. Helping direct your clients and customers to the information and services they may need creates a "need" for you to be part of their real estate transactions. Supplying information about the whole moving and relocation process will endear your services and build loyalty from your customer and client base. In John Tuccillo's book *The Eight New Rules of Real Estate,* John communicates that the value the agent will provide is to save time and eliminate stress for the client or customer. We have the knowledge and experience of the transaction process. We, as consumers, are generally willing to pay for stress reduction on any service. As agents, we have priceless amounts of information. The time is now to change our service model to "extended and continued" service beyond the limits of the transaction.

The new consumer expectations will keep you busy. The key to this litany of new "wants" is the delivery of as many services as possible simultaneously. Your success will revolve around how you design and integrate extra services for your customers; services that extend beyond the basic business of a single real estate transaction. If *you* don't beef up the services, there are hundreds of ways your customer or client will find these value-added services elsewhere.

These services should not be limited to the general real estate arena. With a content-rich database of information about our clients and customers, we have the power to connect our customer base with many of the ancillary services we have previously referred out without tracking or compensation models. Moving companies, warranty companies, inspection services, decorating services, landscaping companies, title companies, etc., are some of the many businesses that have enjoyed our referral business in the past.

The time is now to develop relationships for your own "concierge" style service team to better serve your new client and customer demands. The "single act" agent is a thing of the past, being replaced by "team" services and products. Some of the major companies and franchises are combining services to offer as much to the service module in the transaction as possible. Even if you are not an agent with a huge national company, you can begin to model with your own team of service providers some of the amenities the 21st century consumer is seeking.

The New "Net" Lead

We spend most of our real estate careers prospecting, mailing, networking, and asking for prospects and referrals. The Internet, however, is producing a new type of "lead." The "call-in" of the pre-Web days was neither as informed nor as aware as the consumer of today. Today's consumer can access information at an earlier stage of the decision process. This means that as professionals, we can become involved much earlier in the decision-making process. The good news is that by establishing an earlier relationship, it is more likely we can nurture and sustain a longer, lifetime relationship than previously. The "point of decision," an earlier place in the thought process than the "point of contact," allows us to build lifetime relationships rather than a single experience.

Tracking/Follow-up Systems

The Internet offers us a much earlier opportunity to provide services. However, the prospect is not ready commit at that point; he or she is still in a decision mode. This earlier contact opportunity affords us the connection, but requires consistent follow-up services to expand the relationship to result in a sale and a lifelong client. This is a major reason why the agents today should become proficient with productivity software that automates a seamless follow up to keep the prospect connected to us and our services.

Web sites such as *Homes.com* or *WebSuite.com* offer a template that includes services available on the "back-end." This means the site offers automatic services that are accessible on the Web by your customers or clients online from anywhere, at anytime, via a password. This password allows them to retrieve information for feedback, activity reports, ad schedules, open house schedules, etc. In addition, the Web service offers the ability to send new properties automatically to those prospects listed in the software, as new inventory that meets their needs hits the multiple listing service.

Using this type of automation and a good agent productivity software package, you can count on keeping up with the 24-hour demands of your clients and customers and with the instantaneous changes and inventory in today's marketplace. You can't depend on keeping all the balls bouncing without automated systems to ensure up-to-the-second service for today's savvy client and customer.

Hot Tips to Providing 21st Century Service

Instant Messaging

No more litany of phone numbers to find you; one easy number is all you will need, and all your customers will need to find you. E-mail can be directed to your phone paging system, car, home, office voice mail, car voice mail, portable phone, etc.; all can be directed to one number: you.

E-mail Communication

The newest Web sites offer back-end services that empower you to send, by e-mail, new listing information to a client and customer with full tracking and notification services. E-mail and Web access for communication will replace the old "written" feedback and update reports we have used in the past. Your customer and client will be able to be as up-to-the-minute as you are on the progress of the sale or marketing of the home, complete with reports. E-mail has a built-in urgency for information at the touch of a button. Set yourself up to respond in the way that fits with your service strategies.

Web Site Services

Your Web site can offer immediate information about several different categories of service when you use *linking* (or *framing*) to other informational sources to serve your customer site. See Chapter 5 for the full spectrum of ways to make your Web site work for you and help pay for itself. It is your living "business center" and should be designed to work for you, and without you, 24 hours a day . . . and make you money to boot!

Informational Reports and Updates

Auto responders are the 21st century messaging tools that offer immediate response to information requests. Imagine offering important data in several areas of your digital marketing plan that can meet the insatiable demands of today's consumer. There are many ways for your to offer these immediate informational reports through the new technology applications in the communication software available. Investigate how adding special links in your signature line or on your Web site can help you become a valuable resource to your clients and customers any time they want it, from anywhere, without your immediate attention. Follow up is trackable and manageable, allowing you to maximize the prospecting opportunities of the Web.

Hot Links to Great Service Sites

Get a handle on the newest and greatest Web sites offering customer/client information that you can pass on to your client base. Check out on a regular basis the sites that offer consumer information that you would find of value to your particular farm or community. Check out sites such as *Improvenet.com* (contractor/decorating), *HomeBid.com* (auctions), *HomeGain.com* (agent-seller/buyer match-ups). The list goes on indefinitely. By the time this book hits print, there will be a zillion more. Keep yourself posted by being on mail lists that keep you informed of the latest important information; sites such as *InmanNews.com*, *RealtyTimes.com*, *ConsumerReportsOnline®.org*, and *iSucceed.com™* are designed to provide these timely updates.

Competitive Pricing

E-commerce is forcing competitive pricing. With the coupling of products and services to penetrate lateral markets, many joint ventures were born. The consumer of today is developing an expectation for more competitive angles to attract his or her business. How does this apply to the listing and selling of properties? Think about teaming up with a local decorating service to offer a free decorating session to all new clients that access the coupon on your Web site. A free initial landscaping analysis via a coupon on your Web site or via an e-mail attachment may drive customer action to your landscaper's Web site, making you look great and helping your landscaper create more business as well.

The Wrap

There are many ways that are just developing for the care and nurturing of your new clientele. Anybody can access any of this information for themselves, but SERVICE is always a hot button for today's busy consumer. Let me share an analogy that works for me:

> We all have laundry. We can all do our own laundry, whether at home or at a laundromat. That doesn't mean we want to. We might graciously pay someone a fee for taking care of that service for us ... even though we are totally capable of doing it ourselves.

You need to understand that there is *always* a need for services! People will always pay more for convenience and always pay more for a specialist . . . someone who already knows what *they* don't have the time or inclination to learn. Let that be a thought as you study consumer needs and the ways to fill those needs, as you build your 21st century service model.

Chapter 3

Connecting with Digital Communication

Many of the agents using e-mail think that because they have an e-mail address they have fulfilled their obligations to be "digital." E-mail is only a small part of maximizing the Internet.

"So," you ask, "Why do I need to be on the Internet?" There are a ton of really good solid reasons for you to be connected. Aside from the obvious reason—that it is another way that people communicate and build relationships—perhaps you might like to have other, less obvious reasons, such as passive prospecting. How do you feel about getting leads that are sent directly to you? Would that be of interest to you? There are many reasons, both personal and professional, to join the online community. Read on to find out some of the best reasons to be digital.

Understanding the Service Requirements of the New Digital Consumer

Remember that we talked about the informed consumer? Here is an example of why being connected will make you money. This is a typical phone lead call that I handled just last week that demonstrates why having an understanding of the power of the Internet, both e-mail and a good Web presence, can help you win big time!

This floor call has occurred every day in every real estate office for over 50 years, only this one has the 21st century solution.

> *Terri:* Hi, this is Terri Murphy at ABC Realty. Whom am I speaking with?
>
> *Buyer:* Hi, Terri, my name is John Smith and we are driving past your listing here on Main Street. Can you tell me how much it is?
>
> *Terri:* Yes, that property is a four-bedroom, two-story colonial with a full basement and 2 1/2 baths with a brand new roof and is offered for $234,850. Is that a price range and property description you might be interested in?
>
> *Buyer:* Yes, that is very much what we are looking for. Do you have more information you can send us?
>
> *Terri:* Certainly. Are you working with another agent at this time?
>
> *Buyer:* No, we are just beginning to look and are driving around getting ideas.
>
> *Terri:* I have specialized in this area for over 21 years and would be pleased to help you. I have a full brochure on this property that I can send through the mail, by fax, or via e-mail. Which do you prefer?
>
> *Buyer:* Well, we are flying back home in the next couple of hours and would love the information as soon as possible. Would you send us the information to our e-mail address?
>
> *Terri:* Certainly, may I have your e-mail address please?
>
> *Buyer:* Yes, send it to *Jsmith@MyISP.com*.
>
> *Terri:* No problem. I am sending a full document on the upgrades, complete with photos and room size information. On this particular property, I even have a "virtual tour"

of the home, allowing you to see a tour of the inside of the home as well. By the way, if you want to save time, and want more information about our community, schools, and maps for this area, just go to my Web site and click away. It's all there for you.

Buyer: Great, Terri. I'm impressed that you have your own Web site.

Terri: It's really easy, Mr. Smith. Just go to *www.TerriMurphy.com*. It's all there for you, including a link to my *Realtor®.com* page with all my other listings and listings of homes in our area.

Buyer: That is just great, Terri. I noticed your sign rider with your Web site address on it. That's one of the reasons we called you. Since I travel all the time, I need an agent that can correspond digitally to keep me informed!

Terri: Thank you! By the way, Mr. Smith, have you been qualified with a lender at this point?

Buyer: No, Terri, we just haven't gotten to it yet.

Terri: Let me make it easy for you. Since our area is such a fast market, we would want to be fully prepared if we found the right home and wanted to make an offer. When you go to my Web site, click on the **Loan** button. The company that I'm working with can give us both a prequalification letter and even a mortgage commitment within 15 minutes, all online. Would you find that helpful?

Buyer: That would just be fantastic, since as soon as we get back home, I leave on another overseas trip. This service would just really streamline the work that needs to be done to make our next house-hunting trip more effective. My wife, Jane, and I will review the information after we get in tonight and perhaps ask you to send photos and additional information of other properties that we find interesting. When we get back here next week, we'll be ready to go. Will you be able to schedule some time for us? We have to buy a home in the next two weeks before school starts, and because of my travel schedule I need to keep informed of all the new home prospects that come up in the next few days.

Terri: I would be delighted to find you a home. I'll be confirming our different appointments with a schedule I'll attach to an e-mail. The newest listings that come up will be sent to you via e-mail as well. Then you will have the opportunity to check out the inventory before you arrive. I'll be able to set up our schedule then, based on your preferences.

Buyer: Thanks so much, Terri. We can go back home confident that we will be well informed and taken care of on our next home purchase.

Terri: Glad to help.

Buyer: Thanks, Terri. Jane and I are really looking forward to working with you.

Yep. That's how it went. Would you be ready to offer a full digital solution to this homebuyer? Can you see how this could save you time, postage costs, running time, and long distance phone charges? Read on for more solutions and strategies.

Digital Prospecting

Get ready for the newest and hottest way to prospect for seller and buyer leads! What if these leads could only come to you via your e-mail? *HomeGain.com* is an online homeselling resource center created to match homesellers and buyers with real estate agents. In order to be in the match pool, you need to have e-mail and a competitive Web presence.

The HomeGain site works as follows:

- The homeseller or buyer posts a profile online with information about their requirements and the type of service wanted from an agent.

- The agent must be registered through the Internet on the HomeGain site with pertinent information about his or her area of specialization and sales history.
- The agent receives the profile from the seller or buyer, reviews it, and submits a proposal of his or her services through the *HomeGain.com* service.
- The homeowner compares the agents' proposals, privately and anonymously, in the *HomeGain.com* "Seller or Buyer Control Center."
- The seller or buyer interviews agents by e-mail or a telephone and then meets the best agent or agents in person to discuss their sale or purchase needs.

This site is designed to be agent friendly. It is a resource center created to match homesellers and buyers with real estate agents, saving a ton of time and money in the homeselling/interviewing process. But remember that YOU MUST HAVE AN E-MAIL ADDRESS TO GET NOTIFIED when a seller or a buyer has requested a proposal from agents in their Zip code.

In addition, you will be competing with agents who have a Web site designed with services and tools for a prospective seller or buyer to peruse prior to meeting with you. Your Web presence will need to "sell" you and your electronic presence before you even meet with the prospective homeowner!

According to a survey conducted by HomeGain, the average real estate agent spends between $1,000 and $4,000 to acquire a new home listing. And this doesn't include cold calls, direct mail, and personal marketing. Wouldn't it be nice if you didn't have to work so hard and spend so much to generate new leads?

This matching service for consumers and agents is a great way to get leads sent right to you, digitally and passively! The key, of course, is that you must be connected through e-mail to qualify. There are costs for you to sign up for this service. Since you wait for prospective sellers to contact you, it is a very easy way to generate leads while you are working on something else. For more information go to *www.HomeGain.com*.

E-Mail, the World Wide Web, and E-Commerce

The Internet gives us the option of communicating via e-mail or offering a place to profile graphics and content on a Web site. The combination of these allows us to conduct business by developing e-commerce . . . making money and profits!

In this chapter we'll explain how to get going with even that first baby step to get you on the Internet by explaining the how-to's for e-mail and Internet communication as it is today. The online digital transaction may not be here yet, but it is right around the corner. It's time for us to understand how to restructure ourselves to be relevant to the transaction and why we must be connected to worldwide commerce via the Internet.

The Connection

E-mail offers us communication on the Internet, and can be the most fun. It's just like writing notes in school and passing them around, only this time you do it electronically.

Getting e-mail is easy as long as you have the following:

- Hardware/Software (a computer with a modem)
- Telephone connection
- Internet Service Provider (ISP)
- A little training on "sending" and receiving"
- A bit of online etiquette
- Instruction in how to use your mail manager

The biggest concern for most people initially is getting the whole hardware/software/Internet service program set up and running. Lucky for us, there are good companies out there that will help walk you through the process of getting your computer and you set up to work. (Go to *www.AutomationQuest.com* for a one-stop shop, or check with your local computer tech coaches for sources near you.)

The computer must be "configured" to work with your new ISP, so be sure to have an ISP with a support network to help you set up your hardware/software. (Check Chapter 9 for companies that offer a "full" technology solution.)

There are several steps to creating and promoting your Internet presence. The first step, of course, is to have the hardware, software, and a phone connection to be able to connect to the Internet. You don't need a special dedicated phone line either, just a phone line. Having a separate phone line may make it easier to take phone calls while you are online, but a simple regular phone line is all that is needed to get you connected. The next step is to begin creating your personal presence on the Internet.

The Power of Your Name.com

The highest level identification on the net is a "domain." This means that the name being used is not in a subcategory or part of another account. For personal branding and marketing reasons, *your own name should be your domain name.* Your domain becomes the basis for both your e-mail and Web addresses, and is how people will find you on the Internet. Note my address on the World Wide Web is "MyName.com" or

http://www.TerriMurphy.com

The http://www indicates a Web site address or Universal Resource Locator (URL).

My e-mail address corresponds to my domain name as

Terri@TerriMurphy.com

The "@" sign indicates the e-mail address.

The *TerriMurphy.com* part is the domain, and becomes the core of my entire marketing promotion. *I am my name* in my business. When clients or customers want to buy or sell a home, it is most likely they will find me through some previous marketing efforts of my own, where I have "branded" my marketing tools with my name, photo, slogan, phone numbers, style, etc.

In most cases, people generally remember your name. Add some crazy code name or some butchered version of your name at a particular ISP, and the identification and "memory peg" will be highly diluted.

Register Your Own Domain

There are several steps to getting your own domain. First, remember:

- *E-mail equals the "@" sign.* The part of the Internet where the communication is exchanged, through e-mail, features the "@" sign. An example of an e-mail address is *Terri@ TerriMurphy.com*. The domain part is the "TerriMurphy.com" or "YourName.com." The words in front of the "@" sign denote that this is an e-mail communication going to Terri@ my domain, which is my first name and last name, or TerriMurphy.com
- *Web equals http://www.* The side of the Internet where the World Wide Web resides is where Web site "pages" are viewed. The *http://www* is at the beginning of any Web site address or URL (Universal Resource Locator, if you want the technical jargon).

Here are a few guidelines to direct you down the right road to an ongoing, full, and professional Internet presence:

- Get your own domain by getting your name registered (if it is still available) through a registration service. There are many places on the Internet today that provide name registration services. Check out *NetworkSolutions.com, Register.com,* and others. You can also do this on my own site, *www.TerriMurphy.com*; click on **Resources**. I've set it up to give you value-added service and convenience. ;-)
- It is important that you know there are tricks and traps to this registration thing. I would strongly suggest the services of a professional tech consultant. You can always check with my coach; just go to *www.TerriMurphy.com* and click on the **Tech Coach** button. The price is reasonable for a

15-minute consultation, or more. Otherwise, check with your local board of REALTORS® and ask for their recommended technology consultants in your area.
- Registration is done through a government-regulated Web site and costs about $60–70 per year (and as little as $20! . . . check around), with the first two years paid up front. That fee *does not* include the hosting that will be necessary to have your e-mail forwarded to the ISP of your choice.

Tech Tip

*W*hen hiring a service to register for you, make absolutely sure that you are the owner of your name. Sometimes, the service has been known to register your name under theirs, which means you don't own your own name. For more information on registering your own domain go to *www.TerriMurphy.com* and click on the **Resources** button.

Find a Good Hosting Service

When you have your own domain on the Internet, it is necessary for you to have that domain hosted, to have a forwarding service to direct your e-mail from your domain name to your actual ISP. The hosting service acts as an e-mail forwarding service and charges an annual fee to do so. The fees can really vary, from under $200 per year, or about $16 per month, to $60–$80 per month. Compare prices to be sure you are being charged a competitive price for annual hosting.

Many ISPs won't let you use your own domain without charging you more. They consider a domain more of a "business account." Ask your present ISP what they will charge to host your new domain. In some cases they may tack on anywhere from $30–$60 over and above your monthly dial-up fees for the additional hosting service. An outside hosting service can do the job for you, allowing you to still receive your mail at the ISP of your choice, and in many cases for a smaller monthly fee.

Benefits of Your Own Domain

The good news is that the world will never know if you change ISPs every day or every 10 years, as your e-mail address will not need to change. Should you decide to change ISPs, the decision will be one based on price and/or service. The world will continue to simply send mail to the same permanent e-mail address every time, *You@YourName.com,* avoiding the loss of business or important communications due to a dead e-mail link.

Owning your own domain gives you the flexibility to change your Internet Service Provider anytime you want without the risk of having to change your e-mail address or having to notify the millions of people that have the one you were using.

If you do not own your domain, and if you decide to change your ISP, in almost all cases your e-mail will not be forwarded to a new ISP from your old provider, so the mail will be lost and "bounce" back to the sender as not being deliverable. Loss of business means loss of money!

When you own your own domain you enjoy the freedom of directing your mail to an ISP of your choice at any time by simply notifying your postmaster at the hosting service of the new address where the mail is to be sent for you to receive.

Select an Internet Service Provider

There are different types of ISPs. Web sites such as AOL and Prodigy offer content and connectivity to the Internet. They bring to your attention a number of items, just like a buffet in a restaurant that offers a preselected assortment of items for you to peruse.

These *content providers* have great changing content and opportunities for information exchange, which include fun things such as chat rooms that are part of the perks for belonging as a subscriber to their "club."

These early content sites gave us the ability to "navigate" the Web until the technology developed further to make it easier to "surf" ourselves. Content providers are great at bringing information to us, and more often are designed to provide entertainment.

The other type of Internet Service Provider simply offers Internet connectivity, just like a telephone company offering phone service. With a *business provider,* the only thing you see is pure dial-up service to the Internet, letting you determine where you want to go and what you want to see. The connection offers freedom to go wherever you want on the Internet and does not limit you in any way. As a rule, content providers are great for entertainment, but tougher to use if you are trying to build a professional Internet presence. Choosing a business provider is an important choice in creating a professional Web presence.

CONTENT VERSUS BUSINESS

The Internet offers us the opportunity to conduct business, which generally means there is an exchange of information, documents, etc. In some cases, some of the content providers make it more complicated to attach documents, and often "encrypt" or garble attachments sent from providers outside of their "club."

As a real estate professional, we need to attach many items, like photos, riders, e-mails, etc., without having the problems of encryption.

Another limitation when using a content provider is in the use of your own domain name. It is imperative that you brand your business online and off. In order to keep the branding identification you will want the option of a permanent e-mail address.

Many of the content providers do not allow the use of your own domain (easily), as their goal is to have you "sell" their identification with your e-mail address. So, with a content provider, instead of being able to use *Terri@TerriMurphy.com*, I would be limited to using *Terri@ContentProvider.com.* Sometimes paying extra fees to a content provider can do the trick, but it seems unnecessary to have a content portal when the whole Internet is at your fingertips and a just click away with a business provider.

Simply put, a content provider is great for personal use, but limiting for business applications, along with not sending a full branding message through your e-mail address. Keep your content provider until you have notified your clients and customers of your permanent e-mail address. There are options on America OnLine to reduce your monthly fees to a lower fee based on a time-used basis. As you switch your mail identification over to your permanent e-mail address, you will use your content provider less and less for e-mail and more for the other aspects provided.

With a business provider such as GTE, Mindspring, Earthlink, Global, etc., you make the choices of where you want to go, and you do not have to put up with the tons of advertising, slow service, splash screens, and junk mail that are often associated with content provider sites.

Thus, the argument for choosing a more professional provider for your Internet service. A business provider such as Sprint or AT&T offers a straight Internet connection without the "stuff" found on content sites. No information jumps in your face about the latest scandals, tragedies, etc.; just a pure ISP connection so you can choose where you want to go on the Internet and can use the necessary software you prefer. The costs are about the same, but here are a few of the points to consider when choosing an Internet Service Provider:

- Dependable, reliable Internet connection
- Local dial-up numbers in your area and if you travel

- Space for Web sites
- Space for e-mail boxes and e-mail forwarding
- Affordable monthly payments for unlimited service

Find a company that connects you with a real person to "walk" you through the process of getting your computer configured to work with your new ISP and get you online with a simple click!

Tech Tip

Choose a good business Internet Service Provider for pure and unrestricted access to the Internet; one that offers local dial-up access and has dependable and reliable Internet access for a competitive price.

User Names and Passwords

When you sign up with any Internet Service Provider you will be assigned a user name, which is your account name with this provider. You will also be given (or asked to choose) a password for access when you go online. These are two very important things you need to keep available.

There is a distinct difference between user names and passwords. Your user name is your account name/number. Your password is your code to gain access. Sometimes it is difficult to remember what password you used where, so be sure to have this information clearly written down somewhere. You will need to remember where to find it to refresh your memory!

*T*ech *T*ip

*D*o yourself a really big favor and begin to put all your passwords in one spot. You won't believe how many passwords you will accumulate, and it may be difficult to remember which password is for which service. Start a "little black book" and put them all in it (*as they are written,* meaning upper or lower case as they were assigned and confirmed, and the service they correspond to). You will get passwords for MLS access, ISP access, your company directory access, your lock box access . . . there will be just a ton of them! Keep this list in a secure place. You can thank me later (via e-mail ;-))!

It is important to know the difference between the user name or account name that your ISP will assign you and a permanent e-mail address. Like any new account you open, your ISP will give you a user name that features their name. It will look something like *YourName@YourNewISP.com.*

If you give that address out as your e-mail address, you will begin "labeling" yourself with this account name by selling your (their company) ISP along with your e-mail address. Should you ever change ISPs, this e-mail address will be gone and so, too, will be your e-mail sent to that address.

It is smarter to start out by registering your own name as your e-mail address. This can ensure a nonchanging address, offering consistency to your marketing plan. The good news is you are free to change your ISP any time you feel like it without changing your e-mail address. Remember, you will need your new name domain hosted, which offers the flexibility of using *any* Internet Service Provider at any time without the risk of having to change your e-mail address from *You@YourName.com.* Using your domain name will require hosting, which we described earlier in this chapter. It's worth the monthly hosting fee to brand your name on the Internet and create a strong professional profile.

Don't print up a ton of marketing materials unless you have a permanent e-mail address, or you could be spending a lot of money on printing and reprinting! You will need to keep reading to get the full scoop on this.

Remember that passwords are case sensitive, so however you type your password using upper and lower case, it will always need to be the same.

Tech Tip

*M*ost people new to the Internet don't realize that they have a choice when assigned a user name to use as an e-mail address. Although the user name works, it further identifies your e-mail address with your ISP; not a smart strategy when you are building a "branded" Internet presence around your name.

Now that you have dial-up capability, sending and receiving e-mail is a pretty easy step. You type a message to someone's e-mail address and send it off. Well, it can be done like that, but there is really more to it to maximize this wonderful new medium of communication.

E-Mail: Making It Work for You!

One of the most important points about e-mail is that it is another great communication tool that is far more versatile than a phone or fax. This doesn't mean that you stop making personal phone calls, sending faxes, or writing letters to correspond, it just means you have an alternative mode of communication that has many applications.

This does take a bit of a comfort shift for your normal daily habits, as it hasn't been used by the great masses yet on a regular basis. Here are some great tips about e-mail:

- E-mail is an immediate medium. When you are communicating digitally there is an urgency to respond, since the Internet is impervious to time zones, business hours, or being put on "hold."
- Check your e-mail frequently, depending on the amount of e-mail you send and receive. A good rule of thumb is to check at least in the morning and the evening. For those of us who are heavy e-mail users, checking several times a day might be more appropriate.
- E-mail can be directed to your pager if you are so inclined. Check out the local services available to you.
- E-mail offers attachment capabilities, which allow you to send graphical information as well as reports to increase the efficiency of the communication.

Potential buyers will be sending you e-mail from various home sites, such as *Realtor®.com* or your company site. They are going to expect an "immediate" response. You can't respond several weeks later, as they may have found another savvy agent who handled the lead immediately.

With the probability of sending more and more e-mail daily, there are a few ground rules that will help you save time, energy, and that offer you a brand new way to market yourself through your communications.

Mind Your Manners: Net Etiquette or "Netiquette"

The world of digital communication has a few do's and don'ts for smoother reading and emphasis. There are manners for this new communication medium, called "netiquette." To practice correct digital etiquette, follow these guidelines:

DON'T YELL ON THE INTERNET!

All uppercase words convey to the recipient that you are "SHOUTING" on the Internet. The Internet itself is not case sensitive, so it is appropriate to use uppercase and lowercase when sending a message. Using all lowercase makes things tougher to read and may not convey the posture that you are attempting to convey. Only use all uppercase when you want to make a point and KNOW that you are doing so.

Use Emoticons :-)

The Internet is a somewhat flat medium, so it is not always easy to determine what is meant by words alone. A helpful trick is the use of some symbols—called *emoticons*—to help communicate what you are really intending.

Emoticons give the reader a little more idea of your intention with a message. For instance, if you are trying to be light and friendly, a "smile" can be used at the end of a sentence by using a series of the keyboard keys to make the "face." A smile is accomplished by using a colon : and a dash - and half of a parentheses) for a creation that looks like this: :-) (It helps to turn your head sideways a little to get the full effect.) The same series of keys makes a sad face :-(or a giggle :-))

These useful representations help a message convey the mood and intention of the author, even though the words cannot convey the smile or chuckle intended. Use them in fun and use them often! For more on emoticons, visit *www.chatlist.com*.

Sign Your E-mail Messages

When we send a letter, we expect to sign it. However, many e-mails are sent daily with no name, no signature, and literally no information about the sender. It's not like you can look on the envelope to see where the message came from!

Be sure to "sign" your e-mails by typing in your full name. If you are *not* using a permanent e-mail address and are sporting an ISP account name on your e-mail, it may be difficult to determine from whom your e-mail came. Be sure to include your

- full name
- company name
- designations (if you prefer)
- company phone number and address or town
- company fax number
- e-mail address
- Web address

The next chapter will show you a shortcut to make using your full signature easier, by using mail software to automatically insert your signature at the end of your messages. You may choose to use several different e-mail signatures when using online communication, depending on the purpose. As we use e-mail for both personal and professional purposes, different applications are made easy and convenient by using your e-mail software.

Because it is important to let the recipient know who sent the note, you should provide a clear understanding of who you are. You can design your signature to be user friendly by incorporating a "hot link" to your e-mail and Web site. This adds a touch of convenience for the user, creates a value-added service, and it's a great way to promote your presence! Create a hot link to send you an e-mail by typing the words *mailto* (without a space) followed by a colon to appear like this: *mailto:You@YourName.com*. If your recipient is online, this will hyperlink and appear blue and can easily be "clicked" on to send a ready-addressed message.

Always Use Correct Spelling and Punctuation

Remember, just like a typed hard copy letter, e-mail should appear professional. Typos and misuse of uppercase and lowercase words make your message look like a ransom note instead of a professional communication.

You Are Now Ready

Don't be concerned that we have to discard all the tools that we have been using that have worked so well. The phone is not going to stop ringing and you are not going to sell your fax machine at the next garage sale.

You will continue to print hard copy brochures, hand out your business cards, and put up For Sale signs. By adding your e-mail and Web address (hopefully permanent) to all your marketing materials, you have begun to "brand" your new presence with your standard marketing materials. It's not about discontinuing all those things that have worked for us in the past, but giving them a 21st century look with a new way of communicating with you . . . via the Internet.

The last step is totally up to you. It's just like having a top-of-the-line treadmill in your workout room. You've got to get on it to get in shape! The way to get started is to just "get started" . . . by sending e-mail messages. This is a great reason to call everybody you ever worked with, sold, listed, farmed, etc., and ask for his or her e-mail address. You are on your way to building a strong and viable digital presence!

The Wrap

The most important thing to any business is the place of contact. A business phone number is the way clients and customers reach the service to buy products. Get a permanent e-mail address to avoid changing your "digital phone number" at a later date if you switch Internet Service Providers. Think "globally" and understand that you are your business, so your name should rule! Any name after the "@" sign should be yours, or you are "selling" someone else!

Your name sells "you" in any business that you are in, and is really the basis of your branding to any personal promotion or marketing that you do. This consistency should carry over into your Internet marketing as well. Get your own domain to use both in your e-mail and your Web site address to reinforce the personal branding of yourself and what you do. Your personal name is your identification to the world in your business and personal interactions. So why would you not want to use your own name for e-mail and Web identification? You spend tons of time, energy, and marketing money to attract clients and customers . . . how about keeping you as the star of your own business? Branding is the key, and your name is the brand.

"Branding" is a term you may already be quite familiar with, but perhaps you aren't aware that you are sold by "branding" of merchandise products and services every day. For instance, in the fast-food business, golden arches can only mean "McDonalds." CENTURY 21® created a brand with their gold coats. The Energizer bunny has branded household batteries.

It should be your goal to establish the same reflexive identification with your Internet presence by including your e-mail address and Web site address on all your marketing materials, stationery, business cards, signs, etc. The same notoriety enjoyed by major companies such as Ford and CNN can be yours by "pushing" or leading people to your site, as do the mega companies.

To summarize, remember the following guidelines:

- Use a business Internet Service Provider to help keep you online with a minimum of wasted time and with dependable, reliable, fast service for your Internet needs.
- Practice proper etiquette on the Net when communicating. Be sure you are conveying what you intend to convey by using emoticons to be clear
- Sign all of your e-mails with full signature information. Be sure to include the important "land" information as well as

your digital information. Include your full name, designations, company name, address, phone number, fax, e-mail address, and Web site address. (Check out the next chapter for making this an automatic addition to your e-mail messaging.)
- The Internet is not case sensitive, but passwords are. Be sure to use uppercase and lowercase on the Internet for easier reading, but know the *exact* uppercase and lowercase style used for your passwords.

Some Things to Do Now That You Have Your Own Domain and Permanent E-Mail Address

1. Call all your present clients and customers and give them your new e-mail address. Get theirs for your new database. This gives you a great opportunity to "connect" with them again, and to "push" your clientele to your continued services.
2. Print your new e-mail address on all your marketing materials that currently have your phone and business address. The addition of your Web information to a business card or ad will begin directing traffic to your e-mail and Web address.
3. Expand your print media, such as magazines and newspaper ads, by featuring your e-mail/Web address prominently. Offer additional information as a leader to get traffic going.
4. Begin an electronic newsletter and send out monthly information to everyone in your database.
5. Call your business affiliates (lenders, title reps, home inspectors, appraisers, attorneys, etc.) and give them your new e-mail address. Ask for their e-mail addresses to correspond online and minimize paper communications.
6. Leave a new message on your voice mail that instructs the caller to leave a message or e-mail you at your new e-mail address.

7. Begin using your e-mail for sending showings feedback to your clients.
8. Send new listing information to your sphere of buyers via e-mail and include hot links to sites or properties that might interest them.
9. Get sign riders printed with your e-mail address/URL to promote your Web site and e-mail capabilities.

Tech Tip

The next time you have floor or opportunity time and a prospective customer calls in, ask for his or her e-mail address in addition to the regular info. You create a presence by the very fact that you are asking the question. You will also notice that people have the silliest and goofiest e-mail addresses and that some can't even remember what they are! This is why there is power in having your own permanent e-mail address to create and promote your own personal "brand."

Chapter 4

The Building Blocks of Your Electronic Presence

Being online alone does not create an online personality, thus building an "electronic presence" is key to successfully using technology in your business. The information transfer is just that—information transferred. In order to create an online personality, personal and professional information must be presented in a way that catches the attention of the recipient, and informs the viewer as to who you are, what you do, and where you do it.

In addition, since you are now creating an "electronic business presence" with each communication exchange, there is the challenge of "organizing" this data exchange in a way that provides good service and usable recordkeeping. E-mail communication stretches far beyond sending messages back and forth; the key to building a distinctive online presence involves a few more steps.

E-Mail Managers

It's amazing how many people are using e-mail today! If you ask a large group of e-mail users how many utilize an e-mail manager, most of the group won't be aware that they have one! This is a strong indication that, without using an e-mail manager, most agents are definitely *not* maximizing their mail opportunity to begin building a strong online personality, nor are they seizing the opportunity to use automation to help list and sell properties.

Generally, an e-mail manager is found in the "browser" software. In some cases, your Internet service provider may have provided you a copy of one of the nonintegrated applications, such as Eudora™, as a service to you. If you are using Microsoft Internet Explorer, or have Windows 95/98, the browser is found by clicking on the blue *e* on your desktop.

(The desktop is what comes up after you boot your computer, or turn it on.) If you are online, opening the browser helps you navigate and "interpret" the Internet.

Since there are different versions of Outlook, Outlook Express, and Microsoft Internet Explorer, there might be a few differences in the method of operation, but for the most part they are fairly similar. Netscape, of course, has its own version of an e-mail manager. Check with your tech coach, or use the tutorial offered with any browser.

Here are a few steps to help you get familiar with your e-mail manager. Using Microsoft Internet Explorer (Version 4):

1. Look for the blue *e* on your desktop.
2. Click on the blue *e*; it opens your browser.
3. Scan the top and notice a link that says **Mail**.
4. Click on that **Mail** button and a list menu appears.
5. Click on **Read Mail** and you have opened your mail manager.

Microsoft Internet Explorer offers a brief version of an e-mail manager, generally shipped free in the browser, called Outlook

Express. The full version is also available as separate software, Outlook. This is a great personal productivity tool you can use to begin organizing both online communications and daily life appointments as well. Other e-mail manager applications have similar features and capabilities, such as the ones found in Netscape, or Eudora, etc. Use the one you enjoy the most and that serves your particular needs.

If the browser you are using is Netscape, look for the little box with an *N* in it that looks like this:

N Netscape

Using Netscape (4.0 or greater):

1. Open Netscape.
2. Go to Edit > Preferences > Mail & Newsgroups > Identity.
3. There will be a space to enter in the name of your signature file.
4. Select **Choose**.
5. Highlight the file you created above.
6. Click **Open**, click **OK**.
7. Your default signature in outgoing mail is now set.
8. To check, click **New Message**; your signature should automatically appear.

Automation Saves Time

Your e-mail manager offers hundreds of timesaving services and conveniences. Spend a little time and play with it to explore all the possibilities. We will be highlighting only a few important ones here to get you started communicating like a pro.

E-mail, like any other correspondence, needs to be tracked and filed. It is necessary to begin organizing your e-mail communications electronically. This is done with your e-mail manager.

The e-mail manager will help you file your e-mail electronically, organize your mail with online folders, create a great address book with all the e-mail addresses you "capture," as well as create groups to send mail to. These are just a few options and many convenient services your e-mail manager offers you. Think about taking a Windows course to help you really get up to speed and enjoy more uses of this great software tool.

Make Your E-Mail Signature Automatic and Ready!

Using electronic communication is a very powerful tool and it offers you a strong opportunity to create an online presence. A presence is the way people will perceive you as they read your postings and e-mail messages. Sending e-mail is not just communicating; it is an opportunity to market and "brand" yourself as you begin creating an online presence. For that reason, it makes good sense to maximize every opportunity you get to let the other party know about you, with every piece of e-mail you send. Think globally now instead of locally. People need to know who the sender really is. Giving them additional information about who you are, who you work with or for, and where you are in the universe is not only courteous, it serves many of the customer service principles we have talked about earlier, especially convenience!

The easiest and most powerful way to accomplish this is to set up your signature to be added automatically to each e-mail message. Remember that e-mail is primarily a text medium. While graphics and sound are possible within e-mail, many of your recipients may not receive their e-mail in a manner that allows them to view graphics or listen to sounds. Your "identification" and "personality" come through in several ways, the most important being that the recipient knows who sent the e-mail.

As you know from Chapter 3, many users have not yet learned the power of a permanent e-mail address, and are using cutesy coded e-mail addresses for both personal and professional use.

4 / The Building Blocks of Your Electronic Presence

Here's an example of an e-mail I received recently that doesn't help the recipient (me) know who the sender is (them), where they are from, or what type of communication response is appropriate, business or personal:

Wawcarptr7@vonl.com

If you don't tell us who you are and where you are from, we may have no idea to whom we are responding. In addition, we may accidentally hit the **Delete** button because the sender does not seem to be someone we know. Think of how many regular direct mail envelopes you toss out just by looking at the return address and deciding you don't know the sender; the same applies to e-mail addresses.

Any information that is consistently included in a message needs to be inserted automatically, and this includes your e-mail signature. If you are using Microsoft Internet Explorer's e-mail manager, you can set up your name and vital information to appear without any effort on your part through a series of simple clicks.

Using Microsoft's Internet Explorer as a browser (Version 4.1):

1. Open your browser (the blue *e* on the desktop).
2. When the drop-down menu appears, click on **Mail** and the e-mail manager opens.
3. Click on the tab marked **Tools**, and a drop-down menu appears.
4. Scroll down the menu to **Options**.
5. A series of file tabs appears across the top; choose **Mail Format** (some versions show **Stationery**).
6. Choose the box marked **Signature Picker**.
7. Click **New** and title your signature. Follow the prompts and click **OK** and you are ready.

The next time you click on a new message to send, your signature automatically appears, ready for your message to be included in your e-mail.

$\mathcal{T}$ech $\mathcal{T}$ip

*W*hen you are typing your signature into the signature box, leave a little space at the top of the box before you begin typing your name. This gives you a little room when your signature pops up for the next e-mail and you won't have to move your name down to put in your message. Just a little helpful hint. ;-)

MULTIPURPOSED SIGNATURES

An important thing to note here is that you may need to have several e-mail signatures for different aspects of your personal and professional communication. You can set up additional signatures for as many sides of your life as are appropriate. For example, if you are a committee chair, you may opt to have a signature that features you as the committee chair, and another signature template for your personal communication. Depending on the software you are using, you can develop additional signatures and choose a specific one as a default, which simply means the most-used signature automatically appears, and your alternate choices are set up and just a click away.

YOU ARE NOW COMMUNICATING LIKE A PRO!

A full signature says a lot about you. It offers your name, your company, your designations, your Web site address, your slogan, and possibly a hot link to your e-mail and Web addresses. Be sure to include what you think is important to convey to your recipients. In advanced cases, you might include a link to an auto responder you've set up for a variety of purposes (which we will be getting to in a little bit).

You are now sending e-mail like a pro, looking good, and making a strong impression on everyone who receives your digital communication. In an effort to always provide convenience to all you communicate with, don't forget to include the "embedded link" with your e-mail address for easy return mail. (Remember from Chapter 3 to use the words *mailto:You@YourName.com*.) This will help the novice e-mail recipient who hasn't learned how to capture an e-mail address just yet.

Creating Folders

Your e-mail manager gives you many options to handle your correspondence, including an electronic ability to organize your communications in folders, just as you would with hard copy correspondence. Your e-mail manager offers the ability to name and create "electronic folders" to electronically "file" the information and store all the mail you receive that pertains to a specific subject or property.

Tech Tip

*C*reate an electronic "folder" for each one of your transactions and for prospective customers and clients.

Having a special folder for each transaction makes it easy to keep all the correspondence and information in one spot, and it is easily retrievable without a single piece of paper to misplace! This is also a great closing line in a listing presentation. You can tell the seller that you will be creating an electronic folder for all e-mail correspondence that pertains to this property and it will be digitally organized in your e-mail manager. A great "closing" script at your next listing presentation is: "Mr. and Mrs. Seller, if you are comfortable with our working arrangement, I will set up an electronic folder for all electronic communication and leads related to this property."

Creating a folder is a pretty easy function if you are using Outlook or Outlook Express. Here are your step-by-step instructions using Microsoft Internet Explorer browser (4.1) software:

1. Open the mail manager.
2. Go to **File**.
3. Click on **File** and a drop-down menu appears.
4. Click on **New Folder** and a template opens asking you to name the folder.
5. Fill in the box with the name of the folder (e.g., the address of the property or the name of the client) and click **OK**.
6. The folder now appears on your folder list.

This is a great way to keep track of the volume of e-mail you will begin to receive and make sense of it!

In addition to the electronic file, you may still want to print those letters to have in your hard copy regular file. However, having the correspondence all online makes keeping track of everything a snap. Besides organization, having the folder "archived" (or saved) when the transaction closes is a great way to cover your "assets" should a problem arise later. You won't need to hunt around for that missing "letter" when you know it is in the appropriate place in your computer.

Other Uses for Electronic Folders

As you begin using the full spectrum of e-mail, you may soon see how organizing some of the incoming information is smart and helpful. Some of the folders you may think about creating are:

- Important links
- Past clients

- Mortgage information
- Newsletter tips
- Testimonials (Yes! You will collect them online!)
- Committee information
- Jokes (Lots of them get sent around the Internet)
- Family communication
- Board/Association information
- Prospective hot leads
- Friends
- Passwords
- Billing/Invoices (yes, bill paying becomes electronic!)
- Follow-up by month
- Archiving sent messages

And speaking of archiving, the most important thing you can do with your information is to *back it up*!

Backing Up Your Data

You click on a file and the drive spins and spins and spins. Nothing happens. You've just discovered that your key information is no longer accessible on your computer! If you've backed up your files, this is a minor inconvenience; if not, there's a long night (or day) ahead of you!

Backing up your files is one of the most critical things you can do to safeguard your work and provide you peace of mind. Hardware problems, software crashes, and just plain old human error can create unreadable files and data—usually at the most critical times.

Backups have to be easy, simple, and effective if you are going to do them consistently. If you don't know how to back up, check the information my tech coach put together Appendix A of this book. There are plenty of software solutions for backing up. The key is *be sure to back up often!* (See Appendix A for more information on backing up your data.)

*T*ech *T*ip

*I*f you are unsure at first about backing up your data, hire a tech coach or consultant to do it for you. Better to be safe than sorry. It is worth any investment of money rather than losing your hard-earned information and time!

Capturing E-Mail Addresses

The most important part of any e-mail correspondence is the return address. If you are not familiar with using your e-mail manager, you've been missing just how easy it is to build your address book and contact database with the click of a button, without retyping e-mail addresses!

When using Microsoft's Internet Explorer mail manager (Version 4.1) to add an address to your address book, you can do the following (remember versions may vary):

1. Highlight the name and address of the contact you wish to add to your address book by clicking on it (it is then highlighted).
2. When the name/e-mail address is highlighted, then simply "right" click on the name with your mouse (there are usually two options on a mouse, right and left; this time use the right side); a drop-down menu appears offering you the choice of adding this prospect to your address book.
3. The next template sets up the address contact form automatically with the name and e-mail address in all the right places, with no effort on your part. The best feature is that the e-mail address is correctly inserted, without the possibility of you copying it incorrectly.

4. Save and close. You can begin dividing your data by assigning a category with the mail manager to identify your contacts. As an example, you might want to put all of your past clients in a special "file" in your database, so you can sort for that particular group. Another example is to categorize all clients together, or all personal friends and family in one category. The most important thing is to grab that e-mail address and begin building your electronic database!

Easy and fast and oh, so convenient!

Building Distribution Lists

An e-mail manager gives you the option to build distribution lists. A distribution list offers you the ability to send one e-mail message to a group of people with one easy "group" assignment. The message will actually go to every one of the names in the group, but you are only addressing the message to the group as a single entity, saving time and effort. This is especially helpful when you are addressing a communication to all parties in a real estate contract, your committee, or your special group of friends.

Tech Tip

*C*ollecting, organizing, and customizing your communication with your clients is "data mining," a most important facet of building your business. This new communication tool provides a great opportunity to go back to past clients and customers, get their e-mail addresses, and give them yours! Ask them if they would like you to send them new and current information, as it becomes available. Get "permission," and begin building clients for life.

The organizational purpose of building an electronic database is, by itself, a great move to mastering your marketing and building a strong customer base. However, to plan a surefire "exit" strategy for retirement, relocating to another area, partnering, etc., having your database systematized really makes a transition or transfer easy and professional. (See Chapter 10 on life balance for more info!)

There is a rich value to your database as it applies to ongoing service opportunities beyond the original real estate transaction. This gives new dimension to the theory of "Customers for Life." Use the information in your database to create different profiles that can establish another level of value to each customer. Here's an example:

> You have a customer who has a big tennis interest. You sell this customer a home close to tennis facilities. This extra information detail can be extremely valuable when it is partnered with additional tennis information your past customer is only too glad to have "pushed" to them from you even long after the sale. It shows you are interested and that you can help your customer stay connected to personal interest information.

John Tuccillo, in his book *The Eight New Rules of Real Estate,* refers to this process of taking basic information and combining it with additional database information to create richer profiles. The use of this enriched, personal information can be used to service customers at new levels that exceed the average standard and become a new standard for 21st century consumer expectations.

This reconnection with clients and customers after a sale is one contact we have always tried to accomplish through farming, but now it can be done in a more customized and individualized manner, via a much more sophisticated and meaningful vehicle.

One top agent in California has a most detailed initial interview with her clients and customers. She gets full information regarding the family: ages of children; interests; hobbies; preferences for food, wine, and music; etc. When the time comes to contact a client or customer she has information in her database that is valuable to them, and she can send it electronically or via whichever method she sees fit to make a personal contact.

For example, recently *Consumer Reports* published a report on safe baby walkers. She was able to sort her database of clients and customers with children under two years old to "push" the report about safe baby walkers to the families with small children. Those recipients of this information found it valuable, highly personal, and continue to visit her Web site and respond to her e-newsletters and events.

This highly defined type of contact brings "farming" to a new level. It is highly personal, informative, vital, and of huge personal interest to those who receive the information. This strongly targeted type of information would be difficult to provide without the use of technology and categorization.

With this type of varied and personal information, there is no doubt that you can easily position yourself to become your customers' information center in an ongoing capacity. In addition, this information has value to other companies you may choose to work with to continue to provide value-added services to really keep your client for life. These additional sources of referral information can generate income. Long after the sale, you continue to provide valuable services and information that go beyond the scope of a single real estate transaction and service real life needs and wants.

It works a little like this big corporate deal: Starbucks teams up with a Jacobson's Bagel Store. Both are independent businesses but by sharing different aspects of marketing and customers they can have stronger marketing impact and revenue-sharing opportunities.

Electronic Newsletters

For many years, farming a community or geographical area was done by mailing an area flyers, brochures, or postcards on a regularly scheduled basis. The newest way to communicate, with a minimum of cost at instantaneous speed, is electronic newsletters. Imagine keeping up with all of your past clients and customers with a simple, regular newsletter or update note that is sent by one simple e-mail message. This great tool gives you a timely opportunity to deliver value-added information and ongoing services to any or all of your sphere of influence with minimal efforts and almost no cost.

Electronic newsletter transmissions offer more flexibility than a group distribution done through your mail manager. Newsletter software enables a person to sign up for your newsletter right on your Web site, without your interference or maintenance. Some mail list software programs have you become the "manager" of your own "post office" that handles the subscribing and unsubscribing of those interested in your newsletter. Other software offers capabilities for readers to subscribe and unsubscribe automatically.

Remember in Chapter 2 where we talked about the new challenge in meeting and surpassing consumer demands? Here is the easiest way to supply the major demands in one application. You are serving your customer and client database with refreshed and value-added information in a convenient format. The information you send can be more personally interesting and important to them for use in their daily lives. Your customization of this communication can help drive them back to your Web site continuously after you have already served their real estate needs. (More about this in Chapter 5 on Web sites and the many service and information opportunities you have available.) You'll find us referring to how electronic newsletters work for farming as well in Chapter 6. Check it out later!

Web-Based E-Mail

One of the latest conveniences in e-mail communication is Web-based e-mail. Web e-mail access gives you the opportunity to read and send your e-mail without even having your computer with you! Any access to the Internet allows you to visit your "Web e-mail box" and get your messages.

Kiosks are popping up all over airports and shopping malls, making it easy and convenient to keep in touch digitally. These are the equivalent of a "lemonade stand," only this stand offers you the chance to zip up to the Web and check out your e-mail from any computer anywhere. With Web-accessible e-mail you view and work with your e-mail as it sits on the host server (Internet) before it is downloaded into your computer, allowing you to view your e-mail from anyone's computer or television (using Web TV) that has a connection to the Internet.

Web e-mail is very convenient if you are on the road or not in possession of your computer at the time. You can answer your mail on the Web, keeping that "immediate response" expected with e-mail messaging intact.

Check out getting a Web-accessible e-mail account for yourself, especially if you have e-mail from your own domain! To check if your current e-mail address is Web accessible, go to *http://www.MailStart.com* and do the following:

1. Enter your e-mail address and password.
2. Click on **Check My Mail**.
3. If your e-mail is Web accessible, your messages show up onscreen in a few moments.

Beats hauling the laptop around for those instances where you want to keep in touch but not have the hassle of dragging around the hardware!

Auto Responders: Instant Response Messaging

One of the most cost-effective and flexible communication tools is the technology that allows for an automatic response. This new application is called *auto responder* and is the Internet's answer to what we know as "fax on demand."

A phone voice mail analogy helps us understand how the auto responder actually works. If you are not there, voice mail answers the phone and gives the caller a message. The person placing the call can then leave a message on voice mail.

An auto responder works in the much same way, except the technology returns the e-mail address of the "caller" to you for follow up. An incoming message actually generates an e-mail response from the request for information, and the system captures the sender's e-mail address and shoots it back to you for further follow-up.

When someone sends an e-mail to a special address to request information or a report of some type, an automatic message (which may be written by you) is sent back instantly. The auto responder can respond to hundreds of requests a day from anywhere at anytime.

There are many uses for an auto responder. It can be used to send immediate reports, listing information, vacation messages, community info, etc. In our farming and Web chapters we will show you again the many applications of this great software tool.

An auto responder has a good application for listings. If someone wants information on a brand new listing, they click on the auto responder in the tag line of your automated signature. It might read like this:

Terri Murphy, GRI, CRS, LTG
Top Producer Real Estate Company
http://TerriMurphy.com
mailto:Terri@TerriMurphy.com
Click here for a detailed report for information
mailto:NewProperty@TerriMurphy.com

When the interested party clicks on the hot link to your detailed report, their e-mail manager opens up a new message template and fills in the "to" as *NewProperty@TerriMurphy.com*. They only have to click on **Send** to request the information.

Once that e-mail is sent, the full report goes out to the interested party within seconds. In the meantime, the customer's e-mail address is sent to your account automatically, giving you an instant update and tracking report on who is asking for information. This makes for very cost-effective marketing and makes you more knowledgeable about which advertising publication generates the most activity for the marketing dollar.

It's so easy to use! The recipient does not have to remember any special e-mail addresses. All that is necessary is a simple click on the e-mail link.

An auto responder meets many of today's consumer demands in one easy application. It can work to send out any type of report that helps you list or sell, including:

- Property reports
- New listings
- Frequently Asked Questions (FAQs)
- Confirmation letters
- Brochures
- Detailed articles on your products and services
- Community information
- Testimonials

An auto responder acts like a 24-hour personal assistant, servicing your clients and customers by providing information with an immediate response, offering services or information that meet the instant time line of Internet communications.

How Do You Get an Auto Responder?

You can get an auto responder for a minimum investment (around $150 per year, although this varies) by setting up the account with your hosting service. This is how it works:

- The host sets up a special mail account on their server. You are assigned a special user name and password to gain access to the post office. (I warned you about this password thing, didn't I?)
- Type in the information in a simple e-mail message format right there in the post office, and you are ready to go.

- The report is not limited in size or characters, and you can change the message as many times as you want at any time, without any additional costs at all!

The fees for this automatic e-mail reply service are very affordable. You can use this new auto responder as often as you want, for as many uses as you want. The costs are far less for a whole year than the cost of one ad in the Sunday newspaper!

The auto responder can be demonstrated in a digital listing presentation. (See Chapter 7.) This is where you show the prospective seller how you can create a "detailed report" on the home right at the listing presentation! Most sellers will want to help write the report on the home; a great closing tool. (If you are interested in an auto responder, I've made it easy: go to *http://www.TerriMurphy.com* and click on **Marketing Resources**. My tech coach will set you up!)

Benefits of an Auto Responder

The uses for an auto responder are unlimited, and more ideas are implemented every day! Some of the benefits from using this tool include the ability to

- provide immediate service and information dissemination to an interested prospect;
- change the copy any time you want, as often as you want, for different applications;
- send out detailed reports, hot new listings, reasons to list with you, community information, schedules, etc.;
- reach anyone with Internet access and an e-mail address;
- "close" a listing presentation by having the seller help you "write" the detailed report on the home; and
- capture the e-mail address of the contact requesting the information, offering you an opportunity for follow-up.

Remember, you will see the use of auto responders in several chapters in this book; all are different applications of the same great tool!

Mail Lists or ListServs

In the early days, we spent hours folding, stuffing, licking, stamping, bundling, tabbing, and rubber-banding stacks and stacks of newsletters, flyers, postcards, and whatever to send to our many different farm areas. Whew! It was always a lot of work, with the hope that the mailings would create a "presence" for us in our targeted markets; to "brand" our name and company with the recipient when there was a need for a real estate professional. Lots of work for just hope, wasn't it?

Well, 21st century technology has changed all that! The new communication is a mail list or "ListServ." The Web offers many mail list services. The mail list is an automatic e-mail letter or message that goes out to a list of subscribers, creating a new way to share and disseminate information. Think of this as a special type of e-mail account that sends out a single message or report to a subscribed list of people with one simply typed e-mail message.

There are two types of mail lists we will cover here: one-way and two-way. The one-way mail list gives the publisher (you) the power to send messages to which the receivers can respond. You control the posting of the message to the rest of the mail list. It is designed so the message comes only from you, or is approved by you, before being sent to the rest of the list of subscribers.

The two-way mail list serves a different purpose. With communication flowing two ways, information is shared and the subscribers begin to form an online community that exchanges common interests and information.

For the real estate agent, having a one-way mail list offers the same ability to send farming information to a targeted audience, but without the cost and hassles of traditional mailings, and while maintaining full control of the information that flows through the mail list.

The subject matter, of course, depends on the subscribers. You can have several mail lists that include past clients, present clients and customers, board committees, associations—just about any group that would like to be connected and find information about their common interests valuable.

In Appendix B, you will find samples of newsletters. Study the format and note that a short, simple bit of information that is applicable to clients, customers, and other agents works well. We'll be referring to mail lists in other chapters where you can use them with different applications.

Some Hot Tips on Writing to Your Mail List

1. Keep the subjects short and to the point, using hyperlinks whenever you feel the reader might want more information (link to full articles, etc.).
2. Create a blank template of your newsletter in your word processor and save it as a text file. Keep the line lengths to 60 characters for easy readability and reference.
3. Offer tips on information to appear in your next newsletter.
4. Always ask for comments or suggestions at the tag line of your newsletter.
5. Name your newsletter so that the subscriber knows it is strongly "branded" with your name and heavily associates with you and your services.
6. Use your newsletter to inform the reader of
   - Announcements
   - New hot sites you have found interesting or fun
   - Value-added information about discounts or great services on the Internet
   - New marketing information you have available
   - New tools that are available on your site that would be of interest to the subscriber
   - Neighborhood news
   - Great books
7. Request comments or suggestions from readers for information to be featured.

8. Conduct a poll or questionnaire, and get ideas from the readers, and encourage community.
9. Offer more details about your hot properties with an auto responder built into the newsletter.
10. Offer a report on Frequently Asked Questions (FAQs) about the subject of the month, or a seasonal issue (e.g., taxes, capital gains, mortgages).
11. Get sponsored! Most of the businesses you regularly refer your clients and customers to would be happy to get exposure with a "header" or intro line on your newsletter. Tell them you will feature their company on your newsletter for a period of time for a fee. This will help you pay for your hosting costs.

Chapter 5

Designing Your Web Presence

The Internet offers us a new dimension to marketing and communication as we have known it. As we continue to evolve in this new medium, we know that it offers unlimited networking, instant communication, and global information exchange for a fractional investment of time and money.

As more of the related businesses that service the real estate transaction begin conducting business on the Web, it will be much tougher for the "nonconnected" agent to remain "in the loop," or relevant to the transaction.

In addition, the vast potential for information exchange via the Net has spawned Web sites that offer the consumer access to agents and referral networks exclusively online. If you want to stay in the business without having a Web presence it will be virtually impossible to compete.

A Web presence ensures that you can be accessed and are a part of the network needed to exchange this new level of service information. Without a Web presence, it would be like not having a telephone number or not being in the Yellow Pages and expecting to get business.

It is a strong deviation from how we have successfully practiced our craft for the past 50-plus years. The good news is that the Internet truly can save time, energy, money, and communicates to many at one time, making the job of servicing easier.

The biggest barrier you might be facing now is confusion; fear of how to begin, where to start, and a concern about buying the wrong things! Well, hopefully we can guide you in making those decisions that are the best for you and your type of business.

Choosing What's Right for You

Thousands of Web site opportunities are presented to you every day. So, how are you supposed to choose one, let alone the right one for you? At this point, you don't even know what questions to ask to get all those things that will be right for your personal marketing style, customer market, and personal Internet marketing presence.

What Should I Expect a Web Site to Do for Me?

There are several different types of Web sites, and there are many different uses of a Web site. The first thing is to decide what you expect a Web site to do for you. Consider the following:

- How do I want this Web site to perform for me? Get leads? Profile my credentials and myself? Demonstrate my services?
- What is my target client market (buyers, sellers, business and commercial, vacant land)?
- What is my target location market?
- How much can I invest to develop my Web presence?
- How much can I afford monthly to keep it current and active?
- How interactive do I wish it to be? What type of interactive capabilities am I looking to incorporate?

- Will I incorporate tracking software to determine if this Web site is actually working to get me more business for the investment?
- What is my plan for how I would like my Web site to look? Function? If there are different styles offered, do I know which one I prefer?
- How will I combine my current marketing style with my new electronic Web promotions?
- What organizations and resources do I participate in *now* and already may have paid for that provide Web content for my use? [e.g., memberships in affiliates such as Certified Residential Specialist (CRS), Women's Council of REALTORS® (LTG), local Board of REALTORS®, company franchises]

A Web site should be designed to have several functions. The first function is to provide you an identity or a "living" business center on the World Wide Web. This is why it is so important to have a domain name that is "branded" to you and your name.

We covered the importance of your own domain in Chapter 3. It is very apparent how critical it is for both your Web and e-mail addresses to enjoy symmetry for the highest and easiest marketing recall. So the first step is the same: be sure to secure a domain that reflects your name. This will build your identity for both your Internet personal promotion and your print promotion by reflecting the "branding" of your name in both areas in an identical manner. This symmetry of your name on both your electronic name (*YourName.com*) and address and your printed personal marketing (Your Name) promotions will expand both levels of your marketing to keep the identification directed at you.

Types of Sites

The Web site itself can be one page or several pages deep in design, with the first page referred to as the "home page," and there are different types of Web sites available. The most common is a form of "bulletin board." This is often a one-page site that offers personal information, such as you would find on a business card; basically a type of bio page. The information stays the same and does not offer any changes, as most of us don't change our names, addresses, and phone numbers daily. This single-page site is much like your business card or a Yellow Pages ad, and is generally less expensive than a full, robust information-designed Web site. This type of site gives you a page on the Web, but don't count on having clients and customers visit it several times because there really is no reason to, except to get your phone number or address.

A Web site that offers more value and content, with changing information, is likely to be of more interest and service to those clients and customers you are trying to reach. Remember, as agents we purport to offer 24-hour services. However, most of us really can't be available 24 hours a day, seven days a week, but our Web site can do us a great service by acting as:

- **A Business Information Center.** A 24-hour business information and service center equipped with software tools that extend immediate information at any time to anyone who requests it.
- **A Virtual Assistant.** Your site can be an extension of your office and function as a virtual assistant when it is designed with the information accessible to both global and local clients and customers.
- **An Internet Showcase.** Your Web site can provide a digital dissemination of specific information for clients in a manner that is not restricted to time zones or other time/day limitations.
- **Specific Profile Information.** A site can be created to contain customized information in a manner that is inexpensive and efficient. It can be designed to provide dynamic information that is consistently current and renewed automatically. This is a 21st century answer to stagnant print media that requires reprinting to be updated on a regular basis.

The Keys to Effective Web Planning

The design of your Web site should meet your particular needs and wants, but must serve your clientele as well. We could write a whole book on this information alone. If you are just starting out and want some reasonable and quick guidelines, here are a few important points to incorporate into your Web planning:

- Make it easy to get around on your site. No one wants to wait for big graphics to download or to spend time searching for content buried deep in the site.
- Have the design incorporate easy front-page links to find you and the information that is offered. Design each page with a link to contact you, and make sure it is easy to spot on a page.
- Be sure to design the site to serve your clients and customers. The layout should be consistent with your present marketing by having the same type of "look" on each page to help the customer know they are on the same site as they drill deeper into the site information. If each page looks different, and lacks consistency, you site may be confusing to the viewer.
- There needs to be a benefit and usefulness to visiting your Web site. Take a minute to think about what types of information would appeal to your client/customer base. Information to include might be home improvement information, decorating sites, government loan information, consumer product sites, etc.
- Create a design that promotes interchange between yourself and your visiting clientele. Look for opportunities to incorporate an exchange that offers a risk-free way for people to ask for information or reports. With the use of communication software, such as auto responders, you can consistently extend your product and services to anyone who is interested. Extend invitations to receive your elec-

tronic newsletter for ongoing connectivity. (See Chapter 4 for information about auto responders and mail lists.)
- Extend services above and beyond the norm. This concept is showcased by Nordstrom's Web site, where customers are entertained by piano music. Piano music has nothing to do with retailing, but offers a distinction in service making it more pleasant and different from shopping experiences in other department stores. It also ties into Nordstrom's use of live piano music in its stores. This value-added concept is what our real estate business model is *rapidly* moving toward as we begin to coordinate with affiliate or tandem services. This "concierge" concept of services is being promoted by large companies; it adds that extra level of assistance to the homebuying/selling process. There is no reason you can't develop your own host of concierge services; you can include links to local decorators, landscapers, mortgage and banking services, the chamber of commerce, etc. Consider adding articles that profile these services as an asset to your Web site content; this is the portal concept.
- Link other sites to your site. A good example might be the inventory of housing information; sites such as *Realtor®.com, HomeSeekers,com, Microsoft.com,* or your board or state association aggregate of housing information is a good start.

Many of the listing aggregate sites offer a type of personal Web page on their site for an annual fee. Although they have value and are necessary, few of them are customizable enough to meet your wants and needs for a full Internet marketing presence. Expecting such a page on a major portal site to drive clients and customers to your site may not yield the traffic you had hoped for. Instead, use them as a link to your site, where you offer more services and information that is customized for your clientele. Driving traffic to your own site is more likely to get you contacts than being buried as one of millions in a larger format.

- In addition to personal contact information, make certain to capture other key information from your visitors. For the most effective use of your Web site, have visitors fill out a *short* questionnaire and allow them to prequalify themselves. Prequalification helps you to focus on clients who are really in the market for your services. In addition, offer the opportunity for visitors to sign up for a newsletter that you send out on a regular basis. This allows you to extend your offer of services and information, while providing visitors some sense of connection until they are ready to work with you.
- If you are having a custom site prepared, be sure that the site design does not violate any ARELLO/IRED guidelines. Broker information, code of ethics, fair housing symbols, license information, and disclosure requirements are required in some states. For more information, go to *http://www.arello.org*.

There are literally thousands of important items to consider when buying or building a Web site. There are several templates available; check around and see what appeals to you. Contact your tech coach for questions and answers before investing a lot. Remember that the Internet is brand new and things change every day, so a huge up-front investment may be a waste of your money and time.

Tech Tip

Be aware that having a home page on your company's site or other portal may not be a full Web presence. Company and franchise pages serve the good purpose of locating you and your Web site within a larger site structure, but may not provide as full a Web presence as a site that is powered by your own personal domain address and design.

What's Your Web Address or URL?

You Need Your Own Domain Name

Just as you reflexively go to *Sports.com* for sports, you want your clients and customers to default to *YOU.com* for information and services related to you. The domain plays such a big part in your Internet presence that it is brought up several times in several places in this book, but that's okay . . . you can use the review. ;-)

In order to have a Web site, you need a Web address, or in techie-language a *URL* (Uniform Resource Locator). The format for a Web address is:

http://www.YourName.com

Whatever is in front of the "dot com" is the domain name or Web address of the Web site.

Many agents confuse the fact that they have their own name in front of the "dot com" and think that it is a permanent e-mail address. It is not. Even though your e-mail address is *YourOwnName@Sprint.com*, it is still a temporary e-mail address.

This is where a lot of small business entrepreneurs miss the strongest way to create their own Web presence. The domain is the basis of your e-mail and Web presence, since every way to digitally reach you is designed around this foundational name. You are your business! Mr. Coldwell or Mr. Century doesn't accompany you on listing and selling appointments. You represent the entire corporation as your own businessperson within that corporation or company.

*T*ech *T*ip

*U*nless it is your name before the "dot com" in an e-mail or Web presence, you may not own the domain.

I may be *TerriMurphy@Whatever.com*. If my name is not after the @ sign, I am not an owner or using my domain name. Example: *NBC.com* is selling and positioning the NBC Television Network. If your present Web address is anything but *YourName.com*, you are marketing for some other entity or business—not you—and you risk losing the presence you are trying to create if you ever switch or quit your present Internet Service Provider (ISP).

Choose Your Domain Name Carefully

If you are referred to as Al Jones, then a good domain for you (if it is available) would be *AlJones.com*. If you are known as Allan Jones, then your domain name should be *AllanJones.com*.

Initially, there was a 26-character limitation for domain names on the Internet, which included the dot com. Since then, things have changed; at this writing up to 63 characters are now available. But before you go crazy, determine how your clients and customers will search for or address you on the Internet. The simplest method is your name, or any branding that identifies you and your URL (Web site address) as being the same.

Registering Your Domain (Again)

First, of course, your name or title needs to be available. The number of people registering exclusive use of their names is amazing! That said, it's pretty simple to register a domain these days. To review this info as presented in Chapter 3, to get your own domain you *must* register with a government-regulated site that will license you with the use of your name for a designated period. It will cost you a fee to reserve this exclusive use of your name for an initial two-year period. In order to retain the use of your name, you will need to re-register annually and pay a fee to continue using the license to exclusive use of your name as the domain.

There are several registration sites. This means that there is a central agency regulating the exclusive registration of domain names. You can "purchase" exclusive rights to your name by registering with one of these companies. Up until a year ago, you could easily register a site yourself by going to any registration site and paying the fees, which generally are a two-year registration fee of around $60 and $30 annually thereafter. You can still register a site yourself, but you need to know some key information about where it will reside once you register it. There are some technical issues that need to be filled in. I recommend using the skills and experience of a tech advisor to be sure the process is done correctly.

I've made it easy for you to get registered safely, if you are interested. I've arranged with my tech coach to do it for you via my own Web site. Go to *http://www.TerriMurphy.com* and click on **Marketing Resources** and she'll help you through the rest.

If you prefer to be on your own, visit the following Web sites that will allow you to directly register your site and hold space for you until you decide on a hosting company, thus "reserving" your name before it is gone!

http://www.NetworkSolutions.com
http://www.Register.com

Tech Tip

Be absolutely sure that your name appears for both the billing and administrative contact on the form. This ensures that you in fact "own" your own name for the registered period.

ISP and Hosting Review

In our chapter on e-mail and using your own name as the basis of your Web and e-mail addresses, we talked about how you would still need another service to actually use your name as an e-mail and Web address. That service, if you recall, was "hosting."

An Internet hosting service will "direct" the e-mail addressed to *YourName.com* and forward it to your Internet service provider so that you can retrieve your messages (*Terri@TerriMurphy.com* is directed to *Terri@MyISP.com*). This requires a type of cyberspace post office box to direct e-mail and Web traffic to get to you . . . wherever you are getting your e-mail at the time. The world only knows to send my e-mail to *MyName.com* and my "host" forwards my e-mail to wherever I want it to go.

Some ISPs will host your Web site, but they will charge you an extra fee to do so. It is important to check the monthly or annual fees to be sure they are competitive. Independent hosting services companies will provide hosting services for a monthly fee. A good rule of thumb (at this writing) is somewhere around $25–$60 per month as a competitive range for hosting, depending on the services you wish to have. The more interactive the site, the higher the monthly costs. Automated listings databases, faxing, and other interactivity to your site may be a higher monthly cost. In addition, you will also be paying your regular monthly fee for your ISP connection ($19.95 plus per month).

When searching out a new host for your domain and Web site, the more important considerations include the following:

- Choose a service provider that is a business provider (GTE, Sprint, Earthlink, Global, etc.), and not a content provider (AOL, Prodigy, CompuServe, etc.). Avoid using private networks such as AOL, Prodigy, and CompuServe for a business connection. Get straight connectivity and avoid the limitations of content providers.

    Although the content providers might be fun for personal use, they severely limit your business communications with encryption on attachments and limitations on the use of mail managers, etc. If you presently use a content ISP, and don't wish to lose your e-mail presence by canceling the service, there are ways to reduce your monthly fee to a minimum and keep the old e-mail account until you can direct your e-mail to your new permanent domain. The sender will not need to know who your ISP is, so you won't have to worry about losing mail in the future as long as you keep your registration up on your now permanent domain. There are several tricks to making a comfortable transition, so check with your tech coach or e-mail my tech coach from the link at my domain *http://www.TerriMurphy.com*.

- Be sure that the ISP you choose has local access numbers for Internet dialing at your home/office and in any of the major cities where you plan to travel. Don't pay a long distance charge or an 800-number connection charge for access. Most larger ISPs offer local dial-up numbers for many—but not all—towns across the country.
- Choose an ISP company based on fast connectivity with reliable and dependable service as your first criteria, not just the cost of the service. You can check for ratings on ISPs by location and service at *http://www.isp.com*.
- Select an ISP that offers cable modem and/or Digital Subscriber Line (DSL) connectivity in additional to dial-up access. Having options regarding future connection will enable you to grow with technology instead of changing when direct access becomes more available and affordable. Cable modem and DSL access is now only slightly more expensive than dial-up access in some major metropolitan areas, and the advantages of direct connection versus dial-up are tremendous. Check out the prices in your area for a direct line versus a regular telephone line. As your Web presence grows and your activity with clients on the Internet increases, you'll be looking very seriously at a direct connection option for your primary computer. If you are going to use a dial-up connection, check with your phone company to verify the dial-in number is a non-toll call to reduce your phone charges. Alternatively, select a "call-pack," if available, that provides a reduced per-call rate.

- Check out the amount of "space" the Internet host will allot for the fee. You may eventually want plenty of space to have your Web site hosted; anywhere from 20 to 50 megabytes of space is a good rule of thumb.
- While I advocate having a professional design and manage your site, you may wish to make simple changes directly. Make certain that your site design provides files in formats you are comfortable with (such as Word, WordPerfect, Excel, and Lotus) and that your Web site will work with them. Be sure you have easy access through Web controls.

Other services an Internet host can provide include the following:

- **Unlimited E-Mail Address Capability.** You will want to assign an e-mail address to each and every one of your listings, ads, special projects, direct mail, etc. This will help you to do target marketing and to track your leads.
- **E-Mail Forwarding.** This simply means that you may want to have your ISP provide e-mail forwarding to other ISPs. Here is an example. To create the synergy of *TerriMurphy.com*, I want all of the members of my team to have *TheirName@TerriMurphy.com* as their e-mail addresses. Although my assistant's e-mail address is *Yvonne@TerriMurphy.com*, she actually receives her e-mail at America Online. My clients and customers don't need to know that information. I want to take every opportunity to reinforce the domain name recognition of *TerriMurphy.com*, including having Yvonne's e-mail sent to my domain. My ISP offers me the e-mail forwarding necessary to forward Yvonne's mail to her ISP without cost or interruption.
- **Unlimited FTP Access.** FTP, or File Transfer Protocol, is the way files are transferred from computer to computer. You may not know what to do with it, but if you hire a Web person to do some work for you, you will want to retain access to your site for changes and additions

What Should My Web Site Have?

The first thing necessary to a successful Web site is to develop a personal plan or Web strategy. Simply put, this means you must take time to decide what you would like this electronic business presence to actually do for you. Some things to consider are the style of your Web site, links to other sites, discount offers for visitors to your site, information services, and site tracking.

Style

Do you want people to visit your site for your personal information only? If so, the site you are looking for will function much like a Yellow Pages ad with basic information that does not change. This will not be an expensive investment. However, since such a site is informational only, don't expect to have a large number of visitors, as there are limited reasons to visit this type of site more than once, if ever.

A résumé site such as this will give résumé and bio information and perhaps include a photo and a slogan. This is simply a "digital business card." A résumé Web site is the most limited of sites and provides static information only. If your desire is to have people *return* to your site then read on.

Convenient Links

LINKING FOR CONTENT

If your strategy is to have people visit your site repeatedly, then a different design is imperative to ensure traffic. This means that your Web site design should include constantly changing and updated information that is convenient to retrieve and that encourages a person to visit your site on a more regular basis. This can be accomplished by adding "links" to other Web sites to your site. Here is where you need to do your homework to figure out just what links would be valuable and interesting to your clientele.

A good place to start is to decide what services you can offer automatically that will do for you digitally what you used to do manually. Here's a good example. Often a transferring client is interested in obtaining school information prior to the appointment with you to view houses and neighborhoods. Providing your client with this information requires that you (or your staff) drive to the school, gather the information (assuming the school has current information printed and available), put the information in an envelope, and overnight or mail this information to your customer.

This service is costly to provide in both time and money. It could be done more effectively through your Web site. Here's how. Set up a "link" on your site to the school directory site *ASD.com* (the American School Directory), instruct your customer to go to your Web site and click on the link marked **Schools**, and download the information of their choice at their convenience.

It's this kind of thinking that can help you become more efficient, save money, and "drive" people to your site. And the best part is that you don't have to worry about updating the information; that will be done by the linked site itself. (Note: Getting permission to link to another Web site is a good idea.) You merely link to their site and have no responsibilities or worries to monitor changes in the information; it's always fresh and vital.

Site link information is truly unlimited. Remember, you are now acting as the "center of information" and helping to relieve some of the stress and information overload of your clients and customers. This is where knowing your clientele will help you customize those links and information streams that are desired and targeted for your base of contacts. By investing some time in deciding just what will make the difference, you can really offer a special type of service and set yourself and your services apart from everybody else.

Remember that your goal is to design your site with continuously updated information. If your strategy is to have people visit your site repeatedly for reasons other than your real estate services, you need to offer ongoing creative news and information to maintain their interest level. You conveniently satisfy them by sending them to one place . . . your Web site!

Tech Tip

When linking information from other sites, be aware that there are rules and copyright infringement issues that govern this activity. Consult a professional if you aren't certain how to retrieve this information correctly, or get written permission. A safe way to proceed is to purchase a Web template site that is designed with links already built in.

LINKING TO COMPANION SERVICES

In the 21st century our value to our clientele will be even more defined by the ancillary services we offer during and after the transaction. Design your site to provide links to those companion services you want to recommend. You will be efficiently assisting your clients and placing your services at the top of their list of desirable agents.

This type of "sharing" of your service contacts offers a win-win plan. You maximize service with lateral, zero-based marketing and the outside services enjoy a mini Web presence within your site while branding your name with their client base, as well. This system of "database sharing" empowers you and your service contacts to share and augment the advertising costs that are associated with maintaining a Web site.

Discount Opportunities

The Internet has increased the opportunity approach customers directly (and for customers to seek out vendors and services suppliers), cutting out the middleman. With this has come consumer demand for cheaper pricing and discounts. This new e-commerce model has a major impact on how books are sold (*Amazon.com*), and is now being manifested by consumers' new expanded demands for service, changing forever how business is done.

It might be smart marketing for both you and your service vendors to offer discounts on your site. Instead of offering the traditional closing gift, maybe an online coupon for a complimentary consultation with a decorator might be a useful and unique change. Some agents team up with local merchants to offer discounts on their products or services, or complimentary consultations if the lead is generated from the agent's Web site. This affiliation can be smart thinking and good business!

Information Services for Customers

Would it serve you well to direct clients and prospective customers to your site by offering reports and information? What if this were possible through a type of affordable software that would offer this information at any time, from anywhere, by request, and be automatically sent? If this is a service that interests you, having your Web site set up with auto responders will provide this service for you, while capturing the e-mail address of the person requesting the information. This type of response maximizes the "free" part of accessing information and offers a type of "permission" for you to follow-up. A noncaptured visit to your site is a lost opportunity. Provide a way for your visitors to make contact with you on every page of your Web site. The Internet gives us many ways to "data mine" the responses and offers unlimited prospecting opportunities not available before.

Site Tracking

One of the biggest concerns from agents is that they are not sure what, if anything, their Web site is doing for them. When purchasing a site, ask if the site is designed with site tracking software and the costs that accompany that service. This is a more sophisticated software application than a "counter." Tracking systems vary, but the focus is to be able to use your tracking software to determine where your business is coming from and the effectiveness of your marketing.

It would be important to know, for instance, if you are getting a return on your investment from a banner ad that features you on another site. By checking with your tracking software, you may be surprised to find out you had little activity as a result of this banner. This would help you choose not to continue the expense and to invest your marketing dollar in a more effective ways.

Web Marketing: Your Personal Promotion Strategy

It is common to hear that many agents aren't sure how to promote their Web site and incorporate this new marketing tool into their present marketing strategies. Let's begin with the very first step: directing people to your Web site.

Getting Clients and Customers to Find You On the Internet

How are your clients and customers finding you now? Isn't it true that you use signs, advertising, brochures, business cards, television ads, etc., to attract customers? Your Web site is just another way to attract business. Just like any other type of promotion you do, *you* are the one that directs them there. You are the director of traffic to your own site.

You are the reason people come to you. You have attracted people by your personal promotion and by traditional means that let people know you help to buy and sell homes. The same applies to finding you on the Internet. It's up to you to incorporate the *new* information about your Web site and e-mail into your *standard tried and true* marketing formats.

This might sound very basic, but you wouldn't believe the number of people I have addressed that miss this critical, but basic step:

- Print your (permanent) e-mail and Web addresses on your business cards. Be very careful that this is done properly, as many mistakes have been printed. Don't expect your printer to be Net savvy! Here is an example of how you may choose to have your contact information printed:

Terri Murphy, GRI, CRS, LTG
Broker Associate
Company
Phone Number(s)
E-mail: Terri@TerriMurphy.com
www.TerriMurphy.com

Tech Tip

*P*lease note that I used both uppercase and lowercase for the e-mail and Web addresses. Always type the wording so it is easy to read.

A good friend of mine, Jim Shead, bought his own domain and quickly began using it and creating his personal Web marketing around his name. However, like many of us, he didn't understand that the unprotected areas of the Web are not case sensitive. So he was sending out information that looked like this:

http://www.jimshead.com

If you look at this carefully, you can't quite tell if it says "Jims Head" or "Jim Shead"! An easier way to read his name would be:

http://www.JimShead.com

Don't be afraid to type in uppercase and lowercase unless you are using passwords or are in password protected areas. All passwords must be typed as they were originally submitted. Make it easy to read what you are sending. Use uppercase and lowercase words when sending e-mail! (PS: Jim now uses uppercase and lowercase to let people know it is Jim and not his head sending the note.) ;-)

Search Engines

What, exactly, is a search engine? The simple answer: it's the way to find things on the Internet (with indexes and directories). Yahoo (*http://www.Yahoo.com*), for example, is a search engine that is a directory of well-indexed Web pages. The difference between a directory and an index is that a directory is a listing of categories—like the table of contents in the front of a book—while an index collects "keywords" in a document and puts them together in a list for searching—like the index at the back of a book. Both help you find things on the Internet.

Search engines work best when you know where you are going, which sort of defeats their purpose. Because the Internet is growing so very fast, the whole model for search engines has been forced to grow to help you get where you want to go.

Search engines work in a couple of ways. One way is by "crawling" the Web to search site-to-site to accumulate the information you are seeking. Examples are *Lycos.com* and *Webcrawler.com*. Unfortunately, this method of searching can take a ton of time and may not always produce the results you want. Some search engines allow you to "register" the location of your Web site, which allows indexing of your Web site.

There is plenty of information available about search engines. This technology is changing as you inhale, and by the time you read this new applications will have been developed. XML (eXtensible Markup Language) impacts how we define information on the Net; it allows for a more standardized method for searching all kinds of data. It looks like there will be many changes as the growth of the Internet continues.

The bottom line is don't count on a search engine to do your marketing for you. Even if your prospect uses a search engine it's no more likely that he or she will "stumble" on you (with over a billion Web sites), even if you have a registered site, than it is that your prospect will read the whole Yellow Pages to stumble upon you. The best way to get consumers to your site is to *direct them there through your own personal marketing.*

I personally have never registered with a search engine, and yet if you go to *http://www.GoTo.com* and put "Terri Murphy" in the query box, I will come up about four out of five times. I did not pay or submit any forms to have this happen, so how reliable is the whole search engine concept today?

If you are not going to use your name but some other word set as your domain, search engine registration becomes very important. Keywords and tags that are true indicators of your site content will help to position you in the search engine rankings. It does little good to be listed by a search engine if you are not one of the top fifty in the list. Most people won't explore farther than that unless they are looking for a very specific site.

14 Ways to Direct Traffic to Your Web Site

Here are some great ways to begin integrating your new digital presence with your traditional marketing:

1. Put your e-mail and Web address in your classified and display ads.
2. Buy sign riders displaying your Web address/e-mail address and hang them on your For Sale signs.

3. Feature your e-mail and Web addresses on your brochures and flyers.
4. Include your e-mail and Web addresses on promotional items such as calendars, notepads, magnets, etc.
5. Change your voice mail to include in the message that you can be contacted also by using your e-mail address. Here is a sample script: *"Hi, This is Terri Murphy. I'm not available at this time to answer your call, but please leave a message and I'll get right back to you. You can also send me an e-mail at* Terri@TerriMurphy.com. *I check my e-mail frequently. Thanks and have a great day!"* Be sure to include this in your office, home, and car voice mail too!
6. Invest in the latest pager that can be connected to your e-mail for instant notification. Include your e-mail and Web site address on your direct mail pieces.
7. Be sure to feature your e-mail and Web in all advertising, including billboards, and custom signing.
8. Contact all past buyers and sellers to secure their e-mail addresses and to give them yours, in the event that they need a question answered or need your services.
9. Make certain your staff knows your Web site and e-mail addresses. Have them visit the site and use its features. Encourage their feedback.
10. Contact any organizations you belong to and give them your e-mail and Web addresses, including organizations with whom you have affiliations such as WCR (Women's Council), RS Council (Residential Sales Council), etc.
11. Announce your Web site to your clients with specialized postcards that have your main Web page printed on them. You can get a sample from my site at *TerriMurphy.com* under **Marketing Resources**.
12. Make sure your electronic signature includes your Web address.
13. If your Web site contains a lot of helpful information and links, consider having it published on diskette or CD and

provide it to prospective clients. Include printable coupons to make the info even more valuable. Let *everybody* know how to reach your totally cool digital self!
14. Load your site with good content. A content-intensive site will be designed with links of renewable information to keep the site maintained and updated. It might incorporate links that visitors need everyday and want to be found easily on your site. Links that might be valuable to your clientele include the following:
    - Mapping sites
    - Travel sites
    - Home improvement and decorating sites
    - News and entertainment sites
    - Tax information sites (IRS)
    - Government housing sites (FHA/HUD/VA)
    - Mortgage information
    - Local community information
    - Sports sites (fishing, racing, archery, etc.)
    - Special interest sites (gardening, roses, etc.)
    - Shopping
    - Kids and teens sites
    - Schools
    - Weather
    - Fashion
    - Women's information sites (e.g., I-Village)
    - Historical sites
    - Informational and educational sites (e.g., *National Geographic*)
    - Life and home sites (e.g., Martha Stewart)
    - Kelly Blue Book
    - Consumer sites (e.g., *Consumer Reports*)
    - Financial information sites (Stocks, Bonds, Investments, etc.)
    - Census information

Chapter 6

Farming with 21st Century Communication Tools

If you've been around the real estate industry for any length of time, you have undoubtedly heard the term "farming." Probably you have had your share of collating, folding, stuffing, and rushing to get the date-sensitive material out the door at the right moment for the most impact. In addition, you may have found out it's a good move to make your local postmaster your "best friend." We've delivered more popcorn and sweet treats to our local postmaster, hoping to stay on his "good" side, while sending tons of rubber-banded, color "sticker" sorted piles of direct mail to our different spheres of customers.

Licking, stamping, folding, and often mutilating were a normal part of the 20th century drill to keep your name in front of a customer or past client. We'd stake out "territories" and more often than not, get too busy to keep a regular flow of information, gadgets, gimmicks, and follow-up calls to make the impact required to "own" an area.

Tech Tip

Most electronic messaging can be used as a form of farming

Some of us invested heavily in a regular "premium parade" of spring seeds, summer flags, fall school items, and holiday specialties to keep our presence in front of the targeted group. Magnets, rain hats, pumpkins, and door hangers with recipes or sports schedules were just a few of the many ways we "worked" an area.

The results were directly linked to the regularity of the mailings and its relative importance to the consumer. For the most part, mailers provided self-praising information, which is of relatively little importance to the recipient. If the mailings were consistent but weren't designed with direct response marketing copy, they usually got dumped; perhaps a vague recognition was established. A lot of work for a tenuous connection.

Consistency over long periods of time was a key factor. In addition, the consumer was more interested in personalized value-added information than a package of free seeds. The consumer of today is bombarded with information, some of which is needed and some that is not relative at that moment.

A successful farming strategy is sensitive to

- providing valuable information;
- using direct response marketing to enforce a call to action;
- sending the same marketing piece to build branding recognition at the same time, during designated months; and
- layering personal direct mail with company promotions for greater saturation.

The more successful "farmers" know that a theme systematized with a comprehensive marketing plan is the key to "owning" an area. Unfortunately, many of us have great enthusiasm for farming, but just never carry it to the highest levels.

The Ultimate "Farmer"

Tim Baker, a RE/MAX broker in Naperville, Illinois, chalks up an impressive $43 million in sales volume a year, and for good reason. Well designed and thoroughly executed, Tim has planned his farming approach over a 20-year period to where he now yields a clear profit in the six figures!

Originally, Tim Baker and his wife baked loaves of yummy pumpkin-coconut bread for the 40 homes in the new development where they had just moved. The subdivision was in its early stages and not yet completed. Tim thought this would be a friendly way to introduce himself and his family and begin building a "presence" in the neighborhood. One year later, they were baking 425 loaves of bread and continued to expand the theme; it is carried through his entire personal marketing campaign.

"Never an empty envelope" is Tim's philosophy. A multitude of items, such as kitchen gadgets and premiums, are delivered religiously over six times per year carrying the "Baker" theme.

As the bread demand increased, it took coordination to produce the bread in shifts and allow for same-day delivery. The preannouncement of the bread delivery is done the week before, and the bread is dutifully delivered by kids from church and the neighborhood for a fee. It is a huge success and is anticipated and accepted with great enthusiasm.

Tim continues to maximize the brilliant theme by continuing to feature the "Baker" identification in all materials. Tim's print ads feature him in a photo sporting an apron, mixing bowl, and chef's hat whipping up some bread with a slogan that quips, "Let Tim blend all the ingredients for a good real estate experience." This really reinforces his theme of Baker/Bread, etc., while emphasizing the message through different media and maximizing his market presence.

All Tim's costs and lead calls are carefully tracked to determine if this and any farming activity provides an adequate return on the investment. After 20 years, the bread continues to provide over a 25 percent return and accounts for 47 percent of his business. Today, Tim delivers 6,500 loaves of bread. He never stops working the theme to create more business opportunities. The man has mastered niche marketing and brought farming to a new level of success. Tim offers one of the most cohesive and profitable strategies of niche marketing, farming with a purpose and a profit. His success shows what a well-perfected, traditional farming plan can yield.

Tim is a pretty smart cookie (no pun intended ;-)) and is savvy enough to know that he must begin profiling his new digital presence along with the regular marketing pieces all bearing his e-mail and Web address. Tim sees the new communication tool as another opportunity to connect, along with a phone call and personal contact, while developing a mail list. He has a great opportunity to contact the people in his database, offer his new Web site and electronic newsletter as yet another value-added service, and ask for his contacts' e-mail addresses. Tim is building another layer to an already priceless database. Send Tim referrals at *www.TimBaker.com.*

The New Electronic Farming

In the future, farming will be done via both electronic and print media. It's all about using both the traditional and electronic communication tools branded with all the ways to reach you.

Our databases have a value far beyond being a current report of names and addresses. Databases can make you money when used to send customized *personal* data to your target market. Your customers and/or clients will be delighted at the prospect of having bytes of information that truly interest them delivered right to their e-mail boxes. You are providing a greatly appreciated value-added service, in a convenient way, with the speed that only electronic dissemination offers, and keeping yourself in the position of being your customers' "information center," all at the same time.

New Tools to Use

We already know the value of passing on regular, timely information, as we have done for years with direct mail pieces. Unfortunately, most of the time this information has been related strictly to neighborhood news, statistics, and promoting our recent sales and accomplishments. In addition, using direct mail can be a cumbersome and time-consuming activity, involving the following steps:

- Get current mailing labels
- Affix the labels to envelopes or flyers
- Print the material or newsletter
- Fold, stapling, etc.
- Add enclosures
- Rubber band together
- Sort by ZIP code
- Haul to the post office
- Fill out the forms
- Write the check for the postage
- Hope you made your deadlines
- Wait for the mail to be delivered (time lapse)

If we employed a tracking system, it was limited in scope; it just determined if the business we got was a result of leads from this specific effort. Hard copy direct mail was a form of "broadcast" marketing, to anyone at any given time. In other words, the information was "pushed" indiscriminately to a group of individuals who perhaps had no interest in the generalized information the communication provided.

The new communication tools make it easier to customize the free reports that are of specific interest to your target group. The ease of database selection makes delivery speedy, convenient, and oh so affordable.

Using Mail Lists/ListServs to Farm

We've learned that mail lists/ListServs have several purposes and applications to our communication. We can have a mail list for past clients, new geographic farm areas, or any of the hundreds of applications we can use to build buyer and seller connectivity to us and our ongoing services and information.

As we learned in our e-mail chapter, a mail list (often referred to as a ListServ) is software that sits on your server and acts like a personal post office. Depending on the software, you can be the administrator or "postmaster," "subscribing" people to your mail list. Their e-mail addresses are put into a database of names. The database resides on the server, awaiting a message or report to activate your newsletter message being sent to the list of subscribers.

Unlike a distribution list, covered in Chapter 4, the people on your mail list will receive your e-newsletter as if it was addressed only to them individually. No long and cumbersome list of recipients will show on the message for others to be bothered with or to examine. You simply type or create one e-mail communication message/report/update, etc., address it to your mail list, and hit **Send**. Voila! Everybody on the list gets your message.

Note that electronic newsletters are maximized when they are based on "permission marketing." This means the person has actually asked to receive the information, and you are kindly obliging. Always mail with permission from the recipient or you will be guilty of *spamming*. No one wants junk mail anyway, and especially not on the Internet.

The ListServ method is one of the simplest ways to mass e-mail, since it doesn't take a ton of work to manage and maintain. If someone moves, you simply change his or her e-mail address (if needed). A full distribution group, where all the recipients' names show, takes up space.

There are many advantages to a mail list, especially immediate dissemination of information with instantaneous speed to anyone, anywhere, at any time. The costs are minimal, the time investment the same (or less) as traditional methods, and the rewards are priceless!

How many times would you love to get a chunk of useful information out quickly—about a neighborhood school issue, tax referendum, neighborhood watch, changes in homeowners budgets, etc.—to the people who need to know? A mail list is the complete solution to your needs. Remember the role of the 21st century agent is to provide value-added information and services. Using a mail list/ListServ is a great opportunity to do so. This doesn't mean you should stop sending hard copy direct mail. We are looking for ways to stay relevant to our customer/client base, and doing so in both print and digital media is a great way to go.

MAIL LISTS/LISTSERVS ARE NOT JUST FOR FARMING

One of the challenges to learning about these new communication tools is that there are so many ways to use them. We showed you how an electronic newsletter can be used both as a farming piece and as a means to build a common interest area for those who subscribe to your letter. For instance, if you are farming a subdivision that has a homeowners association, you can be right in the face of every homeowner by offering to sponsor their mail list/listserv and manage the communications. You can do this for less than the cost of printing and mailing one time.

Here's what you do:

- Offer to collect the homeowners' e-mail addresses for the list and, with their permission, subscribe them to the Neighborhood Mail List.
- Develop an information letter that provides guidelines on how to respond to a mail list, the purpose, etc. You might include information about netiquette (see Chapter 3) and the protocol with mail lists (see "How to Be Cool on a Mail List" later in this chapter).
- Set up the list with a "header" showing you as the sponsor. Here's an example: "Sponsored by Your Neighborhood Spe-

cialist, Terri Murphy. For more information go to *Terri@TerriMurphy.com*."
- Close the newsletter with the suggestion that anyone needing services, information, wanting to comment, or wishing to subscribe should respond; give a due date so they know when to expect the next issue of the newsletter.
- Monitor the mail list so it is always appropriate and includes interesting information and viewpoints.
- Have a section that includes upcoming events or other information, such as the July block party, new assessments that are being considered or that will be imposed in the upcoming month, special school schedules, park activity announcements, group garage sales, softball schedules, etc.
- Design the newsletter to have a section that allows the homeowners to list requests for babysitters, summer lawn service, garage sale information, etc.
- Some areas lend themselves well to community projects. One amazing agent started a group to help the elderly keep up their properties during the summer by organizing a "help team" that included kids to help the seniors in their area. He received great recognition, and the results of the kids and adults working together were a great by-product as community spirit was nurtured and developed very positively.

Two Types of Mail Lists

Let's review the types of mail lists again and the protocol and guidelines that go with them.

There are two types of mail lists, one-way and two-way. A one-way mail list is a great solution when communicating with a farm or targeted group of subscribers that is specific, and you wish to control the communication. This means that you are the only one with the power to post to the list. All communication from the list comes directly back to you. If someone responds to your note via your mail list, you will get the e-mail message and the rest of the group won't see it.

A two-way mail list allows a posting to be made to the list, with all members of the list seeing it, and all members free to respond, with all participants able to read all the responses.

When a mail list is used as a two-way communication tool, common interests drive the subscribers to become more united and a community can be built on this sharing of interests. Having a two-way mail list requires monitoring and some ground rules to keep things lively, fresh, and appropriate.

How to Be Cool on a Mail List

Whether you own your own two-way mail list or are a subscriber to other online mail lists, there are some guidelines you might want to know about before jumping right in.

- When you respond on a mail list, you are "posting" your comments, which means your comments are being published. Be sure you offer your full signature, and, like any published piece, be sure your message is checked for spelling, grammar, and punctuation. No room for error here . . . everybody gets the post and you want to create a professional image on line.
- "Lurking" is the term given to those who are on the mail list, read the information, but choose not to respond. Although it is your choice not to respond, being a contributor offers quite a few advantages.
- Contributing to a mail list positions you as an "online personality," exposes you to a great "network," and offers you the opportunity to share your ideas and views.
- Always conduct yourself in a professional manner when responding to a mail list. Never use profanity; the message is out there forever! Incorporate emoticons to make a point if you feel the need to clarify your emotions online.
- If you don't follow the rules of proper communication when posting a response on a mail list, you may receive "negative approval" from other subscribers; this is called

flaming. Resist the impulse to "flame back." Always practice professionalism in any communication, including e-mail.
- When responding to the subject, be clear, concise, and avoid self-promotion. A mail list is a community, not an opportunity for you to promote yourself or your product, unless that is the purpose of the list. Uncontrolled "grandstanding" makes fewer reasons for people to exchange information.
- When replying to a mail list, remember to delete the bulk of the copy and include the material to which you are responding in your response. It is very annoying to have the entire text of the newsletter repeated. It takes forever to load, and is unnecessary. Just "copy" the area you plan on addressing, or delete the rest, and then reply.
- If you want to respond privately to someone on the list, direct the response to that person via their own e-mail address. Note the person's personal e-mail address at the end of his or her post on the mail list and respond to that e-mail address only. Don't hit the **Reply** button within the newsletter; this will direct your private response to the entire list. Following this guideline will save you possible embarrassment and keep your communications between you and the intended recipient.
- When posting to a mail list, make it easy for someone to respond to you privately by including a hot link in your signature with your e-mail and Web address in the signature. It will look something like this:

> Your full name
> *mailto:Yourname@YourName.com*
> *http://www.YourName.com*
> Maybe a phone number and town identification as well

If someone wants to reach you privately, you have just provided information, service, and the convenience to do so. Remember, mail lists are *global*, so no one necessarily knows where you are from or how to reach you.

There are tons of mail merge products available for e-newsletters. By the time this book is published, we may already find that mail list has evolved to a new status. The latest technology allows the whole process to be done on the Web. Who can keep up? Exactly the reason you can be of real value to your sphere of influence . . . because you *do* keep up!

For more information about mail lists, check out "Mr. Internet" Michael Russer's fabulous "e-POWER" seminar, workshops, and his book. For more info go to *http://www.Russer.com*.

Mail List Benefits

Besides the obvious opportunities to save time and money a mail list allows other benefits, including the following:

- Mail lists offer you the ability to "stay connected" in a way that offers value-added information, while keeping a relationship nurtured. That is the objective when we farm in traditional ways. Sending kitchen gadgets has nothing to do with the buying and selling of homes, but it has everything to do with keeping contact in a "service" sort of way.

    This same concept applies when creating content for your mail list. The information in your electronic newsletter should not be limited strictly to "real estate stuff." Interest is created when information is specific to a person's life, and not a glut of good, but perhaps irrelevant, data.

- An e-newsletter can offer you a cornucopia of opportunities to provide interesting, very current, and "customized" tidbits to a specific group of people, designed especially for them. Example: Let's just say you have a neighborhood block party every Fourth of July. Your newsletter becomes information central for the whole group and gives the vital info for the day's agenda.

    If your farm area includes past clients who all have a common interest, say fly fishing, designing a newsletter with new tips, or new fly fishing Web sites offering the latest in fishing gadgets and information, is a valuable way to "push" useful information. This group is only too happy to have the latest info provided and will actually appreciate getting the tidbits in a simple, direct, and easy to use format.

Use E-Farming to Build Prospects

E-mail offers several opportunities for building prospects. Web sites such as *Homes.com* and *Web Suites.com* offer property reports where you can e-mail a listing right from your site. As new listings come online, they are "automatically" e-mailed to a prospective buyer.

The prospect enters the parameters of interest, such as price, size, area, etc., and they are automatically matched as properties become available. Since it seems like you are providing this great service directly, the buyer is "connected" with you on a constant basis until you or the prospect chooses to discontinue. This is so much easier than the old days where you had to mail the newest listings, and keep doing so until you forgot for a while, only to find out the prospect bought from someone else! The prospect and you, the agent, have the ability to "unsubscribe" to the service at any time. This service keeps you connected to the prospect on a regular basis until an interesting property becomes available. I love it . . . technology that makes me look good!

Other farming communication tools available on *Homes.com*, *WebSuite.com*, and others are back-end services that include activity reports, feedback to your clients on property showings, school reports, and even an "on-the-fly" brochure of your listings.

E-Newsletter Reminders

E-mail marketing offers great immediate "connectivity" for farming and client/customer communications. Like any good hard copy newsletter, remember to include the following in your e-newsletter:

- Always include your signature at the end of your newsletter or e-mail message. Keep the signature from becoming too long; a good rule of thumb is six or seven lines total.
- Use a permanent e-mail address and embed the address in your communication and signature line.
- Keep newsletters short and to the point. Use "hot links" for reference to a fuller spectrum of information, to "direct" the recipient if they want more information (e.g., your Web site, special reports, etc.). This is created by adding *http://* and *mailto* (no spaces) to the Web or e-mail address you are referencing.
- Check your e-mail often, but especially more often after releasing an e-mail newsletter. E-mail is an "immediate" medium and people expect you to respond ASAP!
- Build your e-mail database by "capturing" the subscribers' e-mail addresses and adding them to your address book for future follow-up.
- Avoid spamming. No one wants hard copy junk mail, and neither do prospects using e-mail. Avoid "bulk," indiscriminate e-mail. Get permission, and follow the laws in your areas. Spam may be defined differently in various jurisdictions. Consult a professional because penalties are tough!
- Seek out professionally produced e-newsletters. Hobbs & Herder Advertising, Newport Beach, California, does a terrific job of marketing and can help you design a special newsletter for both hard copy and digital dissemination. Check around. There are several preproduced e-newsletters that can make you look great, while providing a great service.

Chapter 7

Selling *You* Before the Listing Appointment

*E*ven with all the digital activity changing how we present ourselves, there is a continual need to use hard copy print, reserved for particular real estate activities. As the new Internet technology integrates its way into our lives, we need to recognize that not all people will be at the same technical level, so be prepared to continue to work in hard copy as well as in a virtual environment.

When you think about it, a listing is just like any job interview. Your goal is to present your personality, skills, and competencies, which in turn convey confidence, organization, planning, and smart marketing.

A prelisting package is one of the surest ways to create a personal distinction in the marketplace and to present a professional image *prior* to your opportunity to meet the property owner.

Hopefully, somewhere in your business plan you have stated that working smarter and not harder is a prime objective. After years of perfecting hundreds of listing presentations, I came to the conclusion that my style and my services might not be for everyone. Nor did I want to waste my time with a homeowner who wasn't highly motivated, or really interested in me at all. I found that I was choosing the properties I wanted to work with as much as the client was choosing me.

I also discovered that by educating the homeowner before the appointment, I was able to alleviate a lot of questions, discussions, and misunderstandings that often develop during the listing period. Any good relationship is built on meeting expectations. Why shouldn't a listing relationship be the same? If both parties understand what they want and expect from the other, the working relationship should be a whole lot easier. But rather than waste my time with appointments that might be unnecessary for one reason or another, I found that "pre-positioning" myself with a declaration of work philosophies and expectations worked very well.

What's the Objective of a Prelisting Package?

I developed my own prelisting package to help position *me* before the listing presentation. My game plan is to inform the homeowner of my intention to maximize the interview time. I accomplish setting the tone by including a cover letter that accompanies the package. The whole package is designed to introduce my team, my mission, and me before I even meet the client.

This preappointment package is designed to send a strong and professional message of my clear intention to seriously market the home. I find that this package helps minimize the occasions I am being "used" to render a marketing opinion, when there is no chance of my getting the listing already promised to a "friend in the business" or a family member.

The prelisting package of information goes far beyond the usual "company collateral." This package informs the seller of the many different services I offer, as well as any I do not normally include. My prelisting package allows me to

- establish a first impression of organization, mission, and introduction;
- include written statements about how I work and what services I expect to deliver;
- explain my full Internet exposure through my Web site and those affiliate sites where I feature property inventory on the World Wide Web;
- provide information about those contractors and service organizations with whom I have established relationships to assist the homeowner;
- state my personal policies and strategies when marketing a property;
- define the types and frequency of communications; and
- educate the sellers as to their role in the marketing process the client can expect (putting the property in top showing condition, the best presentation of furniture, etc.).

The key to the effectiveness of a prelisting package is that it sets you apart from other agents that sellers may plan on interviewing. My goal for this package is to set a precedent of high standards and effectiveness that any other agent will need to duplicate or exceed.

The Key Is In the Delivery

The key to an effective prelisting package is the *delivery*. For local appointments, I try as often as possible to have this full package delivered by a runner or office staffer on the same day that I receive the call from the prospective seller.

A simple receipt is used to verify that the homeowner actually received the package. The receipt accompanies the package, is signed by the homeowner, and returned to our file. The idea behind this is to draw attention to the package and encourage the seller to look it over prior to the meeting. It helps remind me that a package has been delivered, too!

Tech Tip

*G*rab your digital camera and take a photo of the prospective listing. Print it on the envelope that you deliver the prelisting package in. You can bet the packet will get special attention and be very impressive to boot!

Setting the Record Straight: The Letter of Introduction

Just sending the prelisting package isn't enough for me to create the impression I am striving to achieve. I want to set the seller up as to how the interview will work best. The introductory letter included in the package is designed to

- verify the time and date of the meeting;
- ask the seller to peruse the printed material, especially the "Just So You Know How I Work" sheet;
- request that the seller review the "Seller Homework" sheet and have ready for me those things necessary to list the property, including the old plat of survey, title policy, declarations and restrictions, etc.;
- urge the seller to fill out the "Seller Information" sheet for important phone numbers, E-mail addresses, etc.; and
- suggest that the seller view the enclosed videotape (more on this later).

This letter helps the seller understand my time is valuable (as is theirs) and that my intention is to maximize our time together. By having all the paperwork ready, no time will be wasted rummaging through old closing papers trying to locate those items that are necessary and helpful to the listing process.

In addition, the subtle message here is that I am setting an expectation of accomplishment and professionalism, and that I value my time. I have found this step to be the critical one in determining how serious the seller is about marketing the home. The requirements outlined in the letter of introduction communicate that this appointment, for me as an agent, is not a casual one, but an important step in the listing process and should be organized.

How Is the Prelisting Package Organized?

A prelisting package is designed to sell *you* first, then your company and the myriad services that come with your affiliation with that company. As I said earlier, since neither Mr. Coldwell nor Mr. Century ever accompany me to a presentation, I am in fact the full company representative, and it is *me* the sellers are hiring (in most cases). I am the one person representing a gazillion dollar company and the one who will reap the benefit when the listing sells. This means that I need to create the information the seller needs to logically predetermine that I am the correct choice to market the property.

My first priority is to set myself apart from other competing agents who are being interviewed. The secondary goals are to outline clear objectives and my services to help guide the discussion when the seller and I finally meet. Each package is designed to best serve my area and align with my company objectives.

There are many styles of prelisting packages used by top producers across the country: loose-leaf folders, spiral-bound books, three-ring notebooks, etc. Decide what works best for your style and marketplace. The one I use most frequently is easily designed to fit into any company folder with pockets on each side. One side has information about the marketing and the other side has information about me and my personal marketing. You can set yours up in whatever manner works for you. These are just suggestions.

Right Side of the Folder

PERSONAL MISSION STATEMENT

The first sheet is my mission statement, signed by me. This demonstrates to the Seller the fact that I know what my objectives are as a real estate professional. Take some time to develop your own mission statement. A statement of your commitment and objectives will help keep you on track and define your highest purposes for being a real estate professional.

SHOW OFF YOUR WEB PRESENCE!

The second page introduces my Internet presence. It is important for my prospective clients and customers to know that *I am connected!* Since a great percentage of agents have not yet developed their Web strategies, I am immediately set apart by the fact that:

- I have my own Web site, designed with updated information buyers often are seeking
- My site is linked to several other sites that provide convenience, choice, service, and value-added information
- This 24-hour living business center works while I am not, and is integrated with my office and paging system
- I am using the latest technology tools to offer housing and reporting information 24 hours a day and can respond immediately
- I have tracking systems on my site that help target my sources of business and assist me in tailoring my advertising and marketing efforts
- The seller can expect to have this property featured on other Web sites and portals when they list with me

To best highlight my Web presence, I include *screen scrapes* or *screen captures* of my Web site, printed on a color printer. I also enclose screen captures of the company site and any other sites I am profiling in the package. To produce screen captures of Web sites and include them in your prelisting package, take the following steps:

1. Get online.
2. Load the desired Web site.
3. Press the **PrtSc** (Print Screen) key on your computer.
4. Print the page/pages you want to add to your kit.
5. Add to the package with a cover sheet listing the several places where the seller can expect to find this property on the World Wide Web.

GIVE 'EM HOMEWORK!

The next page of the package is what I call "The Seller's Homework Sheet." After 12 years of Catholic schooling, I think the nuns might have had a good idea here. Why not pass it on to your seller? ;-) By having the seller prepared with these items, you can shorten the listing appointment and make better use of your time together. Design this sheet to work in your area. Important items the seller should have ready for your appointment include the following:

- Plat of survey
- Original and last current title policy
- Average of utility bills
- Two sets of keys
- Mortgage information
- Special assessment information
- Special tax information
- List of improvements
- Original tax bill
- Attorney information (some states)
- Phone numbers and alternate numbers (pager, cellular, car)
- E-mail addresses
- Condo/Townhome declarations and restrictions of record
- Homeowner association information
- Homeowner/Condo budget information

The purpose of this sheet is to *not have* your Seller running around compiling this paperwork on *your* time. If you need to take the original documents from the appointment, ask the seller to sign a receipt for what you are taking. This provides you and the seller with a record of what you need to return. Trust me on this one . . . sellers have very short memories and are absolutely sure you "took" everything.

Hot Tip

When dealing with a soon-to-be-transferred homeowner, it is very smart to get copies of the homeowners association documents and covenants *before* the relocation takes place. Having copies in your files saves time and money if the sale occurs during the relocation period. Extra copies of homeowners' documents sometimes cost money and can't get delivered in time for a specific closing date, so do your own homework up front!

THE QUESTIONNAIRE

When I bought my first house, I neglected to ask if the home had a heating system. Consequently, I bought my very first home with no heat (it was in Wisconsin), in a flood plain (so, who knew?), and with minimal insulation (okay, I was really excited about the view and forgot to ask!). It did have a great view. ;-)

The point here is that when any of us are in a selection process, we need to know what questions to ask. Homeowners can use your help in developing a value set, or a set of basic criteria, to compare the services (or nonservices) of agents. You can help them remember the key points with a collection of important questions that you would ask an agent (with unfair knowledge of the services) before securing the services of that agent.

The prelisting package helps set the benchmark for questions by offering to the sellers suggested questions they might want ask when interviewing a prospective agent to market their home.

One of the most referred to sections in the prelisting package comprises a series of questions to help the seller through the interview process when selecting an agent. I call this section "The Complete Seller's Guide." These 20-plus questions are designed for the seller to extract information from an agent and to drive the seller to expect the highest and best services from the person who is awarded the listing. Since most homeowners don't sell their home every day, having criteria for selection of an agent makes the process more comfortable for the seller and more demanding for the agent that can't meet some of the issues the various questions bring to mind. (We've included a copy in the sample prelisting package at the end of this chapter.)

SELL THE TEAM!

If you are a seasoned agent, you may already have your personal team working with you to handle the important administrative work that accompanies the marketing and selling of properties. The seller needs to be aware at the beginning of the relationship who handles what responsibilities, so there is a smooth transition to the right person who handles each task. This avoids concerns later in the relationship and saves you valuable, productive time by directing the service requests to the staff person who specializes in the service.

Even if you are a "newbie" you can still have a team that you work with. Begin with the staff that works in the office. When possible, introduce the seller to the staff that answers the phones, processes the advertising, delegates sign services, etc.

Just because you don't have a personal assistant doesn't mean that you don't have your own "team."

This is also a great place to add the names of the agents who you sometimes "tandem" with to cover each other when one of you is working with another customer or client. This gives the seller the sense that you care about giving service during the times you might not be available. This "back-up" idea works well when you have vacation time or personal days that take you away.

YOUR ANCILLARY SERVICE TEAM

The second part of your team are the contractors and service providers who offer home services. As you begin to refer business to different contractors, landscapers, roof maintenance services, etc., you are in fact building an extensive "team" of value-added services to provide a seller. Choose those people who are dependable and fair in their dealings and who do great work in a reasonable time frame. This group will get plenty of leads from you and will give you repair bids when necessary also. This is a perfect group to include on your Web site as an area of "My Links," if they have a Web site that can be linked.

Some large franchises are offering "concierge" services, which can work just fine. For years I have been able to depend on local contractors who know I will be sending them referrals frequently. I find that their services are value-added referrals that I can offer to clients in need.

Your "B Team" list can include the following:

Painters	Exterminators
Decorators	Asbestos removal services
Landscapers	Radon companies
Pool service companies	Electricians
Snow removal services	Concrete repair companies
Waterproofing companies	Plumbers
Roofing specialists	Handymen
Window replacement firms	Heating/air conditioning firms

Having a team that works with you is a strong asset. Include the phone number and address of each member of your B Team in the packet. Be sure to include a disclaimer at the bottom of each page stating that you are a referral network only and accept no responsibility for the actions or services of those on the list. Have your attorney help you on this one to keep you out of hot water if something doesn't go quite right somewhere down the line.

Tell Them How You Work

One of the most important statements in the prelisting package is the one that defines business strategies and policies. This is the one entry in the package that should be reviewed and signed by the seller. Items to include are dictated by how you personally run your office after the listing is taken, by defining the steps and results the seller can anticipate. By clarifying your services and objectives at the beginning of the listing relationship, you really cut down on the frustrating phone calls that come up later from a confused homeowner. It is timesaving and considerate to take a few extra minutes to explain the "system." I have found it particularly helpful to define the following:

- What happens after the listing is signed
- How the brochures are developed and produced
- How appointments are made
- How agent comments/feedback are given back to the seller (digitally, written, by phone, via e-mail, etc.)
- The policy on business cards after a showing
- The tracking of how many showings to expect before an offer is made
- The responsibilities of the seller to present the property in showing order, including having working utilities and allowing normal access
- How offers are presented and where
- The communication expectations: how often, through what medium (e-mail, phone, written, agent productivity software reports, etc.)

- Advertising policy
- Direct mail policy
- Broker tour policy
- Public open house policies
- Sign policies and placement
- Price changes (I revert to the original listing period time if the seller changes the price during the initial listing period)
- Home inspections: what to expect, who is present, time duration for inspections, and the results of inspections

Some top producers actually print up a card that offers the seller ongoing directions for those items needed in the future. The "Marsha Sell's" team from Atlanta provides the seller with a printed cardboard info card to be placed by the phone. This card lists the phone extensions/direct lines of specific team individuals the homeowner may contact for assistance on restocking of brochures, feedback information, sign issues, etc. It's no wonder that she sells over 40 million a year . . . she is organized, and the seller can get problems solved without calling Marsha every minute.

Get the Seller's Commitment for the Best Way to Present the Home

One of the most important parts of presenting a property is the way it shows to a potential client or customer. Although we don't have total control over the property, it is critical that the seller understands that this is a "tandem" effort. You can't sell a home that isn't in marketable condition. Your favorite department store doesn't wait until you get there to turn on the lights, play great music, and make you feel welcome, and the same applies to a house being offered for sale.

I explain to the seller that we will begin our multipoint marketing campaign as soon as the list of fixes and cleanups is completed. Don't spend a dime or any of your time until the seller has done his or her part. It's your sign on a house that shows like a dump! It takes more than a great marketing team to sell a home; it takes a committed and willing seller as well to make it SOLD!

DEFINE EXPECTATIONS FOR COMMUNICATIONS

The number one consumer complaint from NAR surveys indicates that the homeowner is not satisfied with the communication (meaning the lack thereof) with the agent during the course of the marketing period. Our mission is to "educate" the seller during the listing process so they can better understand and appreciate our work and efforts.

Our mistake is that we assume everyone knows the "process" (how things need to be done). There is a system in every office for how listings are submitted, advertising purchased, open houses scheduled, etc. The key is to let the seller in on how many thousands of details you are handling for them during the marketing process.

The best solution is to implement a "system" that is built around both communication and database information. A good agent productivity software package is your best means to

- keep you organized during and after a transaction;
- cover your "assets" with documentation of services and situations; and
- offer organized database and communication information in one easy integrated application, to save time and make you look great!

For years my favorite agent productivity software package has been TopProducer™. This package offers many different applications for communication for both buyers and sellers. The latest version, System 6i, gives you the ability to download leads directly from your Web site into the new version. Like the previous series, this version includes automatic flyer and brochure software that can save on printing costs. Other agent productivity software packages, such as Agent 2000 or Pat Zaby's products, also help keep you organized. The one to use is the one that you like the best and that serves your needs. Look for a software package that will integrate with the Web to help track and service Internet leads and that works with virtual tour products for flyers and brochures online.

My most frequently used report is the "Market Summary" through TopProducer. I use this report in the prelisting package to demonstrate to the seller how he or she will receive written documentation of completed services showing the time and date they were completed and the person who actually did the work. This has really been a powerful tool, helping the seller feel comfortable about regular communication about the status of the marketing services. You can include the following in this report:

- Advertising dates, times, and publications
- Feedback comments
- Regular services such as sign installation and lock box installation
- Brochure updates
- Broker/Caravan commentary
- Price changes
- Inspection, appraisal, etc.
- Update on Internet leads generated from auto responders, sign riders, e-mail requests, etc.

This is a very strong validation for and explanation of the many details and steps necessary to market a home. I often use this form to document the exact times and dates of phone conversations and faxes sent to confirm actual conversations. This is especially helpful if you have a seller who occasionally gets "amnesia" and forgets the two offers they've turned down or the fact that you just updated them earlier in the week.

You can set up a sample report or just use one from another current client. Either report will help the seller understand that you are in control and well organized to handle the property.

The Wrap on the Right Side of the Folder

So we've completed the right side of your folder. To review, we have included the following:

- Receipt from the seller
- Letter of introduction
- Personal mission statement
- Internet/Web presence information
- "The Seller's Homework Sheet"
- The seller's questionnaire
- Introduction to the team
- The "B Team" list
- "Just So You Know How I Work" statement
- Communication reports

Left Side of the Folder

It's time to direct our attention to filling the other side of the folder with more information for our prelisting package. Fill this pocket with items that will help sell you and the company you work for. These items can include the following:

- Samples or tear sheets of your past advertising in newspapers and magazines
- A printed biography of yourself, including your designations, appointments, awards, etc.
- Company information, including company affiliate services, etc.
- Written testimonials from satisfied customers
- Copies of your past direct mail pieces
- Your real estate office staff information (introduce your manager, office receptionist, ad specialist, closing department, etc.)
- Company magazines featuring their listings
- Special company promotions (e.g., home warranty programs)
- Company volume statistics

- Personal "Preparing Your Home For Sale" checklist
- Your personal volume statistics
- Relocation package information
- Discs with virtual tours with your photo and logo
- Builder list of clients. If you have a list of builders with whom you've done business before, include a list to show you are connected with new construction opportunities as well.

Tech Tip

If you use virtual tours to market your properties, include a sample virtual tour disc of a previous property in your prelisting package. Use a colored label on the disc that features your photo, along with your company name and phone number. This "sells" the homeowner on your extra marketing tools. It's also a great tool to leave in a home for prospective buyers and other agents to take with them after a showing. A full virtual tour works better than a flyer when time is at a premium and adds to your multifaceted marketing plan.

Hot Tip

Superstar producer Terry Paranych, a top producer from Edmonton, Canada, uses a "Table of Contents" in his prelisting package. He produces a printed booklet of about 40 pages and uses his prelisting package as his actual listing presentation. His costs (including delivery) are about $8 per book. For more info on his prelisting package and others, visit the *iSucceed.com* training site at *http://www.iSucceed.com*.

I have examined prelisting packages from several top producing agents. All of the styles and forms are just terrific and are, in most cases, highly successful and very detailed. There are many additional items you could add to this packet. Your job is to determine what works in your market for your clientele. The important thing to note is that you are the representative that they are hiring. Take the time and spend the money to create professional looking pieces and reproductions of the collateral you will include. Be careful not to put too much "company" stuff in there or the customer will think the "company" did it, not you. Personalize the package so clients know exactly who and what they are getting.

The prelisting package should offer the strongest, most professional impact on a prospective seller. It is crafted to profile *you* as the *right choice* for marketing the home. Listen to your market; study it to find out what your clientele is looking for and include what you have found out in your services. The idea is to educate the seller, using your personal profile and marketing information, before you get there. Don't include a market analysis, but include a tax information sheet if it is appropriate. We love letting the seller know we've done our homework!

Other Things You Can Add to Your Prelisting Package

Make a Move to Include the Kids

If the client has children, I include my Clean Kids Club membership form. This is a great way to get the kids involved in the move and to let the parents know you are aware of the kids' involvement in the process. I give the kids an opportunity to be a part of the selling and marketing effort by offering to enroll them in my Clean Kids Club.

This form is simply a certificate made with a decorative piece of stationery. My choice is the "Star Performers" sheet. It is colorful and has a large area of white space in the middle.

In the middle of this sheet of paper is the declaration that "Little Tommy" is now a part of helping keep his home (especially his room) in top showing condition, thus becoming a valuable member of the selling team. For the child's efforts, a couple of McDonalds gift certificates are included as a weekly or monthly benefit for his efforts. I also like to make it more "official" looking by affixing a gold notary starburst with my CRS designation imprinted on the seal. Very impressive! (See the sample at the end of this chapter.)

This certificate is best delivered through the U.S. Postal Service, in a plain envelope (not company) that is decorated with fun stickers and hand-addressed to the child. It makes quite an impact and takes on a tone of being a more official message that the kids are part of the team effort. I often find this certificate is proudly displayed on the family bulletin board or refrigerator. The parent(s) enjoy the recognition of the children, and the kids love the "award" aspect of the program.

VIDEO "TRAINING" AND INFORMATIONAL TAPES

One of the key routes to credibility is to have the direction come from a recognized authority. Even though traditionally I had used a seller's condition checklist, I found that sometimes that just wasn't enough. I then added a videotape to the prelisting package. My intention is to help the Seller help me sell their home. David Knox, an industry leader, produces a series of great videos to help us out.

The tape I have chosen, *Pricing Your Home to Sell,* has David addressing the seller about the perils of overpricing the home at the initial marketing. David's unique approach to helping the homeowner understand the damage done to the marketing process by overpricing the property makes him the authority. You are less of a bad guy when you deliver the message of price reality after completing your market analysis work.

David's tape is a most professional way to set you up to deliver an accurate reporting of a Comparative Market Analysis on the home. This tool has helped many of us get the seller into the mindset to market the property in a reasonable price range. To get copies of David's videos, phone him at (800) 533-4494 or e-mail him at *Info@DavidKnox.com*. Visit his Web site at *www.DavidKnox.com* for more information on these great selling tools!

You might want to purchase several copies of this tape. Be sure to devise a system to pick them up after the presentations to keep your "library" intact. The investment in this tape can help the homeowner understand pricing and save you lots of time, energy, and money. Setting up pricing information early in the listing period helps when facing a disgruntled seller later in the marketing period. The worst scenario is handling the marketing through the "overpriced period" only to have the listing expire and be picked up by the next agent who sells the home quickly at a new, more realistic price.

After the listing agreement is signed, I deliver a second tape in the Knox Seminar series, *Preparing Your Home to Sell*. This video gives the homeowner instructions on what to do to maximize the "showability" of the home. David does a great job offering suggestions and tips to the homeowner for the best way to present the property.

Hot Tip

Keep this video under wraps until after the seller has signed the listing agreement! No need to help a competitor by setting up the seller to show the home right . . . make it your job!

Advanced agents include information in their prelisting package on their homebuying programs, exchange programs, and statistics on how many homes they sell an hour, a day, or a week. They also include testimonial pictures and statements, tips on selling, and information about cancellation of a listing agreement. Decide what is appropriate for you and what meets your company's policies and objectives.

Other items top agents include in their prelisting packages include the following:

- Personal guarantee programs
- Seller equity balance sheets
- Copies of special advertising campaigns
- Information about agent owned moving van services
- Moving box services supplied by agents
- Photos of happy homeowners with testimonials

Think Creatively

The purpose of the prelisting package is to define and sell and your areas of expertise, to set you apart from other agents being considered for the listing. Begin to think about those services that would be of value to your client or customer.

When you finally meet at your scheduled appointment, your client will have a lot more information about you than about the other agents he or she plans to interview. Your professionalism and dedication to helping the seller ask the right questions and explaining the process is often welcome. Remember to take the time at a listing presentation to walk the homeowner through the process to alleviate confusion and disappointment later.

The Digital Listing Presentation: The Next Step

The next chapter covers the latest ways to demonstrate to the homeowner your great new presentation! I will discuss how I have incorporated many of the written pieces used in the prelisting package to produce a PowerPoint presentation.

The Integrity Factor:
Your Internet Marketing Strategy

People respond best when they know the objectives of any relationship, be it business or personal. Establishing guidelines and setting goals help sellers clarify their expectations about your services. You need to develop a marketing strategy that incorporates both the traditional steps and the new Internet strategies you plan to provide for marketing your properties. This written strategy also provides an impressive organized solution to the quandary of what exactly this Internet stuff is going to do for the seller, and particularly what you plan on doing to maximize its effectiveness.

Having this strategy in writing has proven to be the key to setting me apart from the gaggle of other agents the seller might be interviewing who may not be as "tech savvy" as I am.

Tech Tip

Put your marketing strategy on your Web site. This is especially helpful if you have the opportunity to work with relocation companies or lead-generation sites that refer prospects to your Web site for information about you.

If your listing presentation is a "two-step" type, it might be very beneficial for you to reserve offering a hard copy of your Internet marketing strategy to the Seller before you do your final listing presentation. Review it at the time of your meeting, but leaving a copy may help the seller to "quiz" the next agent. Using my strategy as a model, the homeowner is now interviewing the other agent with my marketing plan. When asked most agents might simply respond, "We offer that service as well." Even though the strategy is available on your Web site, the homeowner may not check the site prior to your meeting.

I don't mind helping out the other guy, but I reserve my special services and customized strategy until the seller actually signs the agreement. Then I submit the written report with what has already been completed and what is on schedule. This presents an organized, efficient, and written validation of the services that I promise to offer and that my promises are actually being kept.

The Wrap

The strongest validation to your professional integrity is to *do what you say you were going to do* and report those services back. Using an agent productivity software package is most helpful for validating dates, times, and services performed for a client or customer. Some of the latest Web sites offer back-end services that also help track communication and services rendered during the marketing process. Whatever the system, use the following guidelines to serve your client:

- Tell the client what you are going to do.
- Do everything you say you were going to do in a *timely* fashion.
- Report back in writing the fulfillment of those services. . . . Just do it!

Terri Murphy's

Prelisting Package

TERRI MURPHY & ASSOCIATES
Selling Homes Faster for More Money!

RECEIPT

As the:

    ___ Designated Agent of Seller
    ___ Designated Agent for Buyer
    ___ Seller
    ___ Buyer
    ___ Other

I HEREBY ACKNOWLEDGE RECEIPT OF THE FOLLOWING:

_____
_____
_____

RE: SELLER _____ BUYER _____

        PROPERTY _____

_____
(SIGNATURE)

_____   _____
(PRINTED NAME)   COMPANY, IF ANY

DATE: _____

TIME: _____

Terri Murphy & Associates
P.O. Box 6234
Libertyville, IL 60048
Phone: 847-367-8699
Fax: 847-367-8753
E-Mail: Terri@TerriMurphy.com

OUR PERSONAL MISSION STATEMENT

TO LEAD THE INDUSTRY IN DEMONSTRATING SUPERIOR SERVICE AND TO EXTEND EXTRAORDINARY COMMITMENT TO THOSE WE SERVE IN THE REAL ESTATE INDUSTRY.

Terri Murphy & Team

Terri Murphy & Associates
P.O. Box 6234
Libertyville, IL 60048
Phone: 847-367-8699
Fax: 847-367-8753
E-Mail: Terri@TerriMurphy.com

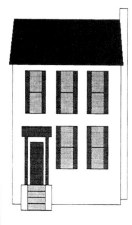

Visit Us at Our Web Sites

www.TerriMurphy.com

www.CBChicagoland.com

www.Realtor.com

www.ColdwellBanker.com

www.Cyberhomes.com

Terri Murphy's listings are accessible through the World Wide Web via several sources. We can provide 24-hour advertising and information services via our virtual office on the Internet for global exposure to market your home.

Individuals who visit our Web site and want more information on listings can do so through our e-mail listing information software. Prospects can secure an immediate e-mail report of the actual listing with a virtual tour, when available. We do include the offer to send hard copy information upon request.

We also incorporate on our site the latest communication tools such as auto responders and mail lists for instant response capability. The software is designed to notify us of the request for information. We can then immediately respond with additional information and follow-up services.

Terri Murphy & Associates
P.O. Box 6234
Libertyville, IL 60048
Phone: 847-367-8699
Fax: 847-367-8753
E-Mail: Terri@TerriMurphy.com

Marketing Proposal for the Property at:

In addition to the Seller's Guarantee, offered through Coldwell Banker, the following items are added to the marketing for Terri Murphy's clients:

INTERNET PRESENCE
The property is submitted to the Multiple Listing Service of Northern Illinois, and will enjoy additional exposure through the following Web sites:

 www.Realtor.com   www.ColdwellBanker.com
 www.CBChicagoland.com   www.Cyberhomes.com
 www.USAToday.com   www.TerriMurphy.com.

 Realtor.com is the official Web site of the National Association of Realtors®, enjoying over 179 views per property per month and an aggregate of 1.3 million listings. Realtor.com has exclusive agreements with USA Today, NBC, AOL Digital City, and Classifieds2000, with 80 major sites. Terri Murphy has a Realtor.com Homepage Plus, providing immediate e-mail capabilities for inquiries on the property and the ability to host three different photos of the property instead of one. Additional information is available on the property, along with hot links to Terri's interactive Web site at www.TerriMurphy.com. As an added feature, Terri's web presence is expanded by links to ColdwellBanker.com, CBChicagoland.com, Yahoo's weather site, the U.S. Census Bureau, ADS School Directory, a mapping service, and other local and community information resources. At each and every opportunity there is the capability of an immediate, direct e-mail link to Terri through her own Internet domain at Terri@TerriMurphy.com. This Web presence and immediate communication capability has helped Terri achieve status in the top 1 percent of Realtors® across the country and solidifies the 21 years of top producer performance.

COLDWELL BANKER NETWORK

Coldwell Banker Chicago offers a network of 1,700 licensed sales agents that work on a referral basis for both listing and selling to encourage sales within the company. Coldwell Banker's acquisition of two prominent North Shore companies, Kahn Realty and Cyrus Realty, has increased both prominence and sales in the immediate area of the North Shore. In addition, the acquisition of Prudential-Burnett has garnered the Coldwell Banker team strong market share of the Lake County area.

ADVERTISING

Coldwell Banker offers a monthly statewide publication, *The Buyer's Guide* (sample attached), which offers an expansive level of exposure through the print media in a guide designed to sell homes. The media publications most used on a regular basis are the *Chicago Tribune, Chicago Sun Times,* and the *Pioneer Press.* Coldwell Banker spent over $1.8 million on print media in 1999 and continues to lead the industry in excellent print and media exposure. For executive level properties, the prestigious *Previews* is an option with statewide circulation.

VIRTUAL TOURS

Terri and her team employ the latest marketing for virtual tours of her homes. This allows for a "walk-through" of the home on the Web with full 360-degree views of the property both inside and out. These tours are accessible on her iLead pages for REALTOR.com, ColdwellBanker.com, and CBChicagoland.com

AUTO RESPONDERS AND DETAILED REPORTS

Terri provides immediate communication by implementing an 21st century "fax on demand" response through mail software that can offer information on your property to potential buyers literally on demand. The software offers 24-hour access and immediately disseminates the information. Simultaneously, the prospective buyer's e-mail address is directed to Terri's mail manager, and a phone call follow-up is provided for additional service and information.

TERRI MURPHY'S TEAM

In addition to Stevie and Jeff Clark, Paul Jacobson, and Scott Flesch, Terri has staff available during business hours Monday through Friday. Yvonne Drewanz staffs the office as a licensed assistant. Terri offers a direct line for her personal clients and customers, a 24-hour private fax line, a 24-hour permanent e-mail address, and a 24-hour interactive live Web site. Terri is also part of the Coldwell Banker Libertyville office team managed by Colleen Fleming.

UPDATES AND COMMUNICATION

Terri believes in the automated office and implements networked computer software programs that integrate the details and many steps required to effectively market a home. Her software choice is Top Producer®, which offers a weekly summary and update of activities that have been completed and initiated throughout the marketing process. These progress reports are mailed or faxed every 10 days during the marketing period.

Feedback is secured from agents that have shown the property on Mondays, Tuesdays, and Wednesdays, and are communicated to the seller no later than Thursday. 1999 statistics show that in order to secure one feedback commentary from an agent, a series of 6.7 phone calls are required. Since Monday through Wednesday are broker/agent tour days, and given the lack of cooperation from buyer brokers, it is not possible to deliver the comments back to the Seller before the end of the week. Other arrangements can be made if required.

BROCHURE PRODUCTION AND DISSEMINATION

Terri's over 21 years of experience has indicated that a fact sheet should be on premises in the home for the benefit of the buyer and the buyer's agent. Since multiple listing sheets are oversimplified, providing insufficient information about upgrades and inclusions, material profiling the property more substantially needs to be available. Terri's staff takes photos and creates a brochure that is reviewed by the seller prior to printing and should be completed within the first week of the listing. An acrylic holder is provided to the homeowner to display the brochures. A total of 30 brochures are targeted for in home showings. The average number of showings-to-sale for 1999 was 17.5, given the correct pricing pocket and average availability of similar housing.

DIRECT MAIL

Coldwell Banker's art department has designed a direct mail postcard for Terri announcing the availability of new offerings. Homes are grouped according to use and pricing to effect the highest call response. Additional mailings are scheduled to agents both in the North Shore area and in the top producing pockets of the Lake County area.

Terri Murphy's marketing does not include public open houses unless requested and negotiated with the seller and other marketing services provided with the listing. Those properties requiring special showing services are determined on an individual basis.

_____   _____
Terri Murphy   Homeowner

Date: _____   Date: _____

Terri Murphy & Associates
P.O. Box 6234
Libertyville, IL 60048
Phone: 847-367-8699
Fax: 847-367-8753
E-Mail: Terri@TerriMurphy.com

SELLER'S HOMEWORK

Please supply original or copies of the following:

__ Original and last title policy

__ Survey

__ Mortgage paperwork

__ Latest tax bill

__ Declarations/Covenants (if applicable)

__ Average utilities

__ Information on specific assessments (if applicable)

__ Residential Real Property Disclosure Report

__ Addendum to Seller's Exclusive Marketing Agreement

__ Copy of Personal Holiday/Christmas Mailing List

__ Two Keys for Front Door and Deadbolt

__ E-Mail Address(s)_____

__ Signed "Just So You Know How We Work" Explanation

__ Homeowners/Association information – Amount $_____

Company and Address:

Contact:

Terri Murphy & Associates
P.O. Box 6234
Libertyville, IL 60048
Phone: 847-367-8699
Fax: 847-367-8753
E-Mail: Terri@TerriMurphy.com

THE COMPLETE SELLER'S GUIDE
To Interviewing a Real Estate Broker
To Market and Sell Your Property

When interviewing an agent, understand what services they offer and what services you are interested in. The following questions are designed to tell you if the agent is taking the listing for reasons other than getting your property SOLD!

1. Do you work as a full-time REALTOR®?
2. Do you have a full-time assistant?
3. In what area and in what aspect of the market do you specialize?
4. Do you have a written marketing plan specifically designed to sell my house?
5. Do you attend local, state, and national REALTOR® meetings? How often?
6. How often do you market properties directly to buyers?
7. How many properties have you sold in the last three (3) months?
8. Will you produce a professional flyer about my home with a picture displaying my home?
9. Do you have a written business plan and mission statement?
10. How often will I hear from you after my home is listed with you? May I cancel the listing if I don't hear from you on a scheduled basis?
11. What software do you use to track the activities to market my home?

12. How do you find potential buyers? Do you have a system to identify potential buyers?
13. What other marketing techniques will you use to get my property sold?
14. In what ways do you encourage other realtors to sell my property? How do you network? Do you work with affiliates? RS Council? Women's Council?
15. What can I do to help sell my property?
16. How many listings do you have? What percentages of them sell? In the past?
17. Do you have an internal marketing plan? Please describe it.
18. Do you have a personal Web site? The address is _____
19. Do you have a permanent e-mail address?
20. What presence have you developed through your marketing?
21. Does your company have a Web site? The address is _____
22. Who does your Web site link to?
23. Do you have listings on REALTOR®.com?
24. Do you have a REALTOR®.com home page?
25. Does it link to your personal Web site or home page?
26. Do you have a list of references I can call?
27. What automated communication tools do you use for 24-hour access and service?
28. Do you have a database of qualified buyers for my home?
29. Does your Web site offer automated services for feedback, activity reports, and updated market analysis information I can secure via the Web?

*Adapted from Walter Sanford, Sanford Group Incorporated

Terri Murphy & Associates
P.O. Box 6234
Libertyville, IL 60048
Phone: 847-367-8699
Fax: 847-367-8753
E-Mail: Terri@TerriMurphy.com

JUST SO YOU KNOW HOW WE WORK...

Thank you for the opportunity to let us market your home. In order for us to properly market your home, we must work together. This sheet will let you know how Terri & your personal team works for you.

Pictures. The picture of your home for Multiple Listing Services is taken by the multiple listing service. Our staff photographer takes our own brochure photo as weather permits for best results. Three to five days should be allowed for processing.

Our photos are *digital photographs* for use in brochures as well as electronic marketing. Virtual tour shots are ordered when applicable. E-gallery's are often used as property promotional options and as links to virtual tours on Terri's Web site and other sites in order to provide 24-hour exposure to your property.

Internet Upload. The upload of information about your property to the Internet (to REALTOR.com and our company site, for example) is not immediate, as it is for our local Multiple Listing Service. Please allow a few days for the information to be uploaded from the local MLS. Also, be advised that there is a strict limitation on the space available for copy, which is why Terri uses the expanded options available on other Web sites.

Brochure. A brochure about your home will be produced by our staff. This brochure will highlight any upgrades and improvements to your home and will include local information about schools, taxes, and amenities. If there is information that you would like featured in this brochure, please be sure to notify us right away. The brochure will be completed as soon as a satisfactory photo is produced and we have received from you the approved copy for printing. Upon

Prelisting Package **143**

approval of the content, the brochure will be printed. Note that we cannot make any changes until the next print run. We allow for thirty copies, which should be more than sufficient. Please notify Yvonne at our office when/if you need more brochures.

Feedback. Feedback from other agents showing your property are secured daily and delivered to you on a weekly basis. **You, the seller, will be called on Thursday or Friday and the feedback will be given to you verbally.** In the event that you cannot be reached, a message will be left on your voice mail or E-mail. We are very open to making any other arrangements that work for you.

Top Producer®. Top Producer® is a sophisticated software program that we integrate into our business communications and tracking services. The program is designed to track activity on your property and supply you with a report of those activities. During the marketing process of your property, we will provide you with this essential information and also keep an accurate accounting of all activities, which include showings, feedback from those showings, connections from our database those potential buyers that desire the property needs that your property may accommodate. Most beneficial is the ability to analyze the market and your property together, giving you, the client, the most current market information available.

Advertising. Your home will be advertised a minimum of twice during a listing period. Terri's proven media of choice is the *Chicago Tribune, Pioneer Press,* and *The Daily Herald.* For executive-level properties, we also offer a special direct mail service with Coldwell Banker Executive Preview Services as well as Chicagoland exposure for Premier level properties.

Direct Mail Services. Coldwell Banker has an in-house Direct Mail Service Division. Our annual marketing strategy is designed to send out a minimum of 5,000 pieces of direct mail per month to targeted markets for property exposure. The targeted market is determined by geography, database, market dates, lead generation, etc.

Showcasing Your Home. Terri and staff will "stage" your home after we have an agreement to work together. This service includes a staging tape for you to review and Terri's own personal critiques. Terri will offer tips on how to make the property show more attractively, highlighting the property and not your personal belongings. You can begin by packing up those objects that are not necessary for daily living; items that may make the home look smaller are more cluttered.

Utilities. On vacant properties or before closing on your current property, utilities must be available and in working order. Walk-throughs must be done with utilities on, and they must be on for visits by agents, prospective buyers, and home inspectors.

Showings. Showings help us sell your home! Please make every effort to have your home ready and available to show at reasonable times. An electronic lock box will be placed on your door to make your home more accessible for showings and to electronically track showings. The box will remain on the home until after closing to accommodate the final walk-throughs and home inspections. We also prefer to keep a key in our office until the property has closed.

Price Changes. In the event that the market activity reflects a need to change the listing price of your home, the listing agreement date will automatically be extended for the original length of the listing period (e.g., 90 days, 120 days).

Offers. We prefer to present any offers in Terri's office with both brokers present. Terri's office provides the copies, teleconferencing, riders, and forms that may be necessary. Faxing is used when time and opportunity make it necessary.

Inspections. Home inspections can take up to three hours. Often the buying party will accompany the inspector during that time. The buyer pays for this service, and only the buyer's agent will be present with the buyers during the inspection.

Concierge Services. Any services that are recommended by us are done so only on an informational basis, and are offered strictly as a convenience. We cannot accept responsibility thereafter; however, we are always interested in feedback and comments.

Public Open Houses. It is our policy to discourage public access to our properties to those unqualified buyers and/or nonserious prospects through public open houses. We have listed and sold over 100 properties per year without the use of this system. We are much more comfortable knowing the motivation and purchase power of a prospective buyer prior to exposing your home, family, and personal belongings to complete strangers. If you are still in favor of public access, we will discuss those options with you.

Staff Services. Our staff includes Yvonne Drewanz as Director of Operations. If you have any questions about the listing process, open house, or other general questions, please contact Yvonne. Scott Flesch heads our buyers' team to coordinate all showing opportunities and to work with prospective customers.

Closing Services. As an additional service, we are pleased to deliver information to your attorney. However, we are not responsible for these items.

We are here to provide the finest service available. Please let us share your ideas if we can be of further service! Thank you!!!

We request your signature on the line below so that we know we have presented to you all the avenues we use in marketing your property.

_____   _____
SIGNATURE OF CLIENT   DATE

Terri Murphy & Associates
P.O. Box 6234
Libertyville, IL 60048
Phone: 847-367-8699
Fax: 847-367-8753
E-Mail: Terri@TerriMurphy.com

Meet Terri Murphy's Team

Terri Murphy has earned Top Producer status as she developed her 21-year career. Listing and selling over 100 properties per year for the past 21 years, she defines herself with a high commitment to professionalism and cutting edge services. Having earned a Graduate of the Real Estate Institute (GRI), the Certified Residential Specialist Designation (CRS), and the Leadership Training Graduate Degree from the Women's Council of Realtors, Terri comes equipped and focused to the arena of listing and selling properties. Her book, *Listing & Selling Secrets*, published by Dearborn Publishing in 1995, is number 26 on the *Amazon.com* list for real estate books. Her newest book, *E-Listing & E-Selling Secrets for the Technologically Clueless*, will be published in the fall.

Buyer Agents Team. Terri and her team work closely with several hand chosen top producing agents that primarily service buyers and buyer leads. With Terri's interactive, content rich Web site, the lead generation from auto responders, mail lists, and information extracted from our site tracking and Web management software, many buyer inquiries are generated. In an effort to maximize all services, traditional and digital, Terri has teamed with Scott Flesch, Donna Sears, and Connie Catharine in her immediate office to handle all inquiries.

In addition Terri's team is expanded by her 20-year career partnership with Stevie Clark, the Coldwell Banker Top Producing Agent for northern Illinois and her team of Paul Jacobson that service the North Shore. Stevie's son, Jeff Clark, teams with the group to service the northwest suburban areas out of the Buffalo Grove office and handles far west areas such as Crystal Lake and Algonquin. This simply means we provide our customers and clients with the highest quality of service and immediate follow-up with any lead without bringing dual agency into play.

Yvonne Drewanz functions as our office assistant and handles feedback communication with other agents while tracking showing progress for our clients. This enables us to "read" the market on a daily basis to consistently study the position of the property on a regular basis and to assess the property's position vis-à-vis new and pending properties as they enter the market as a competitive entity. Other agent feedback helps us to correct issues that are concerns of prospective buyers to help define our marketing efforts while yielding shorter marketing periods and pushing the boundaries for higher dollar offers per property.

Mortgage Services. Provident Mortgage, based in Libertyville, has always provided our clients and customers with current competitive mortgage information. We are able to prequalify our buyers, even during nonbusiness hours.

Sign Services. Terri's "For Sale" signs and riders are contracted out to a professional placement company, Liam Gallup. The Gallup Company is responsible for the sign, its maintenance, and all sign riders. All orders come through Yvonne Drewanz. If you need assistance, please call and let us know.

Contractor Services. Terri has recommended the services of Terry Molnar of Heritage Renovations, a trusted Libertyville professional. Terry offers his services to her clients and customers for tasks such as repairs, remodeling, recarpeting, and repaining. Should you need this type of service, please consult the B-Team list for those contractors and services who have worked with Terri over the years and have her endorsement.

Terri Murphy & Associates
P.O. Box 6234
Libertyville, IL 60048
Phone: 847-367-8699
Fax: 847-367-8753
E-Mail: Terri@TerriMurphy.com

THE B-TEAM

In order to prepare your home for market exposure, here is a list of affiliates and concierge level services to assist homeowners and new buyers.

ATTORNEYS

Thomas F. Meyer (847) 295-0070
33 N. Waukegan Road
Suite 105
Lake Bluff, IL 60044

Don Kahn (847) 367-6095
150 E. Cook Avenue
Libertyville, IL 60048

Carole Madden (847) 367-5404
1117 S. Milwaukee Ave.
Libertyville, IL 60048

CLEANING

Metropolitan Cleaning Services (847) 367-8500
729 E. Park Avenue
Libertyville, IL 60048
Bill Hughes

American Maid (847) 263-6153
Waukegan, IL
Pat Buse

ELECTRICAL

Howard Electric (847) 438-2232
15 Highview
Hawthorn Woods, IL 60047
Kevin Matczynski

LANDSCAPING/LAWN CARE
  Casey Nursery & Landscaping   (847) 367-8188
  28320 Hill Top Terrace
  Mundelein, IL 60060
  Ken Chapin

DECORATOR
  Susan Sassetti Interiors   (847) 367-1064
  Libertyville, IL 60048

HOME INSPECTOR
  Bill Moss   (847) 918-8001

WELL AND SEPTIC
  John Rayber   (815) 344-4020

HEATING & AIR CONDITIONING
  Oelerich Heating and Air   (847) 566-7900

WATER PROBLEMS
  Dependable Water Proofing   (847) 356-8452

BASEMENT CRACKS AND LEAKS
  Dura Shield   (847) 381-5717

CONTRACTOR
  Terry Molnar – Heritage Renovations   (847) 680-0942

CARPET CLEANING
  BIG KAT Carpet Cleaning   (847) 949-8112

RADON TESTING
  VSI Environmental Service   (847) 740-7730

APPLIANCE SERVICE
  All Star Appliance Service   (847) 223-3383

MOVING SERVICE
  Shurway Movers   (847) 362-2976

These services are recommendations for informational purposes only. We accept no liability.

Terri Murphy & Associates
P.O. Box 6234
Libertyville, IL 60048
Phone: 847-367-8699
Fax: 847-367-8753
E-Mail: Terri@TerriMurphy.com

As a REALTOR®, Terri Murphy and the Murphy Team provide you with these benefits when selling your home:

- As a licensed agent for 21 years in the Lake County area, Terri and her team are dedicated to getting top value for your property. You deserve top value in the marketplace for your property, but determining the pricing pocket *at the time of the marketing* is the key. Our team is dedicated to professionally analyze the current marketplace to determine the fair market value of your home on a consistent basis to meet a changing market.

- The Terri Murphy team is heavily involved in an extensive referral network. Using our agent productivity software program, TopProducer™, we have a pool of preapproved and motivated buyers waiting for the right home to match to your property for a quick and effective transaction.

- With over 21 years in the Lake County area, we are experts on the local community and surrounding areas. It is part of our REALTOR® responsibility to be knowledgeable about schools, shopping, public transportation, churches, social clubs, and other amenities offered by our community. Knowledge is the power, coupled with information, to save time and the stress of relocating to an area.

- The Murphy team is open to finding the right property for their customer, in an unbiased way. This offers full informational services about any and all properties that are suitable to any buyer at any time.

- Our precision marketing exposure provides strong and targeted marketing expertise, using all media. With Terri Murphy's full interactive virtual offices on the World Wide Web we offer global exposure, with 24-hour advertising and information access. As part of our business, we know how to market your property through the best available media, including other REALTORS®.

- The Terri Murphy team is trained to offer suggestions that enhance the marketability of your home. With the team's expertise, we can help you make your home more desirable to different kinds of prospective buyers. We will provide a source for contractor bids to help make the decisions that affect the marketing and appeal of the home compared to similar properties on the market.

- The Murphy team extends our services even after a buyer is secured. Through developed networks in the industry, we understand the legal and financial requirements of a home sale. Our B-Team of ancillary professionals provides an additional network of proven professionals to assist your individual legal, financial, and personal needs.

- Our team can help alleviate the stress of closing the transaction. Our professionally trained team has worked together with a full agenda of closing items to be handled prior to your occupancy. We will work with your attorney/title company to facilitate a seamless transition of ownership.

- An agent concerned with all of your real estate needs encompasses the services of a professional consultant. Terri and her team extend professional consulting services to serve all aspects of your real estate needs.

Terri Murphy & Associates
P.O. Box 6234
Libertyville, IL 60048
Phone: 847-367-8699
Fax: 847-367-8753
E-Mail: Terri@TerriMurphy.com

Builders Client List

Companies we have worked with for new construction homes

Atkinson Builders - Joe Atkinson	847-680-8187
Avis Development - Mike Avis	847-913-0600
Calanca Construction - Neil Calanca	847-362-3567
Century Bay Builders - Jack Shaver	847-680-1869
Davis Development & Design - Bruce Davis	847-680-4114
Family Builders - Lita Matczynski	847-438-8530
Frank Guido Construction - Frank Guido	847-356-1942
Homes By Michael Lloyd - Michael Libert	847-369-3433
Oakwood Group - Shaver & Kuchar	847-680-8148
Orrin Pickell Development - Orren Pickell	847-816-7773
Suburban Realty Development - Samual Libert	847-771-4545
Traditional Homes - Ray Truelson	847-634-4950
Potesta Quality Custom Homes - Mark Potesta	847-247-9638
D.R. Weiss Custom Homes - Dennis Weiss	708-443-9600

Terri Murphy & Associates
P.O. Box 6234
Libertyville, IL 60048
Phone: 847-367-8699
Fax: 847-367-8753
E-Mail: Terri@TerriMurphy.com

SELLER'S ESTIMATED EXPENSES

Property Address: _____ Date: _____

Estimated Selling Price . . . . $ _____

Less:

1. Unpaid balance of mortgage $ _____
2. Mortgage prepayment penalty $ _____
3. Unpaid tax prorations to buyer $ _____
   (Seller may have funds in escrow, which would offset this expense)
4. Attorney's fees $ _____
5. Seller's title charges (estimate) $ _____
6. Deed tax stamps $ _____
   ($1.50 per thousand)
7. Village tax stamp $ _____
8. Survey $ _____
9. Brokerage fee and closing fee $ _____
10. FHA or VA Discount, if any $ _____
11. Inspections (well, septic, termite) $ _____

   Total of Expenses: $ _____

*Estimated Cash to Seller: $ _____

*Estimated costs and charges only

Extras You Can Include In Your Package

Other items to consider adding to your Prelisting Package include the following:

- Testimonial letters from satisfied clients and customers
- Copies of your direct mail and report on results
- Copies of your advertising collateral
- Special company programs that offer value, such as warranty programs, guaranteed sale programs, advertising budget information, listing tips, pricing information, and special provisions for easy exit of listing agreements (per company policy)
- Unique advertising programs, such as moving vans, billboards, bus benches or other outdoor advertising, broadcast or cable television ads, and radio advertising or personal radio presentations
- Photos of your team
- Information about your buyer systems
- Personal biographical information that is *useful* to the consumer, such as language specialization, market segment specialization, expertise in certain types of financing, and specialization in property types (e.g., farms, rural, ranches, oceanfront, foreclosures, senior housing)

Chapter 8

An e-Look for Your Next Listing Presentation

In the "old" days, a good flip chart or presentation book did the job and demonstrated to any captive homeseller the reasons why a particular agent or company was the perfect choice to professionally market his or her home.

Things have changed. The consumer is more sophisticated. Newly equipped with a broader understanding of the choices that are available via the World Wide Web, the homeowner can be more selective. Service, as it was once defined (deliver the goods with a smile, on time, at the right price), is not the only key to getting and keeping any relationship or account. Indeed, good service should be a "given" in any vendor-client relationship.

As I've said repeatedly, you must now meet a higher level of client expectation than ever before, just to get the client. The expanded list of expectations for "service" now includes delivering convenience, among other things. Since the Internet provides information on a 24-hour basis, consumers now drive the purchase of products or services in their own time, at their own pace, and quite possibly at their own price.

The information available through the Internet helps consumers make a decision about a desired product or service with a much clearer understanding of the choices and quality being offered than ever before. With a little work, comparative values are analyzed against quality, pricing, discounts, and convenience. These new consumer demands move at a faster, 21st century pace as well. The consumer of today wants it all: services, information, and less stress, with great pricing whenever and wherever possible.

This new palette of demands changes how we demonstrate our products and services. Technicolor used to be new and exciting. Now Laser and DVD have raised the expectations of the average consumer to the point that advertising and presentations are expected to be full graphic productions.

What does this all mean to the real estate agent trying to win buyers and sellers? It's taking more to dazzle the 21st century consumer. National statistics tell us the average homebuyer is 34.7 years old and comfortable with a computer. The time has come to learn the newest ways to present our services in a fresh, crisp, updated way that incorporates our traditional marketing and interfaces with the newest technology and Internet communications.

Get the Digital Edge

In the past, we employed flip charts and personal display books to convey to the seller that it was smart to hire us. Complex graphs and glossies previously demonstrated our strong market share, affiliate programs, and other ancillary services designed to impress the homeowner.

The old tools did their job when the world wasn't changing in a nanosecond; they did help the seller visualize the positive aspects about you, your company, and the marketing being offered. However, the 21st century consumer is more savvy and thereforedemanding. This consumer has a new set of criteria to decide what aspects of service they want from an agent. They are often more technologically sophisticated than the average agent, which is why you may need to have a digital edge to impress, compete, and win.

Technology and its applications change at the speed of thought today, and printed collateral materials alone cannot compete with information that can be profiled and changed digitally. It's imperative to begin incorporating the tools that can help you win, not just compete, in the listing and selling marketplace. It will take a few tools, but all of them are worth far more than the investment.

Get a Laptop Computer

The virtual office is the name of the game. The agent of today needs to have all the tools and information available in all buyer and seller situations. Besides freeing the agent from a desk, the laptop computer allows the agent to have a full spectrum of presentation programs, agent productivity software, and communication tools all in one place. The virtual office can offer today's agent flexibility in all phases of managing and growing the business.

Learn to Use Presentation Software for Listing Interviews

For a nice digital presentation, Microsoft PowerPoint is a favorite and works well; it allows immediate customization for each presentation. Another choice is Top Presenter®, a Top Producer product. Other agent software demonstration programs are now available. A well-planned digital presentation incorporates the same information you have been offering previously, but featured in digital images, clip art, and text on a screen for a more interesting and versatile presentation. Whichever software you choose, use the one that works the best for you and that you are comfortable demonstrating.

Use Screen Captures

Avoid having to "get online" at the appointment. By using screen captures, you are not dependent on Internet connectivity that can interrupt family phone lines or that can experience difficulty with Internet access at the "critical" time.

Using screen captures provides the seller a preview of what you have and how it looks in a less time-consuming way, without distractions or technical glitches that can complicate your presentation. Try to use your battery power instead of having to use power cords. Simpler is better, especially if there are children and pets around.

Customize Your Presentation with Tech Tools

To really get attention, open the presentation with a screen that features a digital photo of the seller's home. Not only will the seller be delighted to see this personalization of your presentation, but this also indicates that you, the agent, are versatile at using other digital tools, such as the new digital camera, in your marketing.

Subsequent screens can be used to set up the interview with the information you have been outlining in your hard copy presentation. Define the objectives you will address in your presentation and use tools to help your seller visualize your products and services. It may be a good idea to have a printed copy of your presentation to leave with the property owner *after* you've received the authorization to list the property. The seller may need to refer to it at a later date.

Components of an Electronic Listing Presentation

Just like a personalized prelisting package (discussed in Chapter 7), your electronic listing presentation should reflect what you want to communicate to your clients and customers. The balance of this chapter describes screens that can be used when discussing your marketing strategy and demonstrating your objectives and services in your marketing presentation.

Web Sites Where the Home Will Be Featured

Show the seller Internet sites where his or her home will be featured (URLs). Any homeowner will be interested to know the many places the home will be featured. Copy the company Web site home page and other related sites that feature listings. There are several sites offering home information, the best known being *Realtor.com, HomeAdvisor.com, HomeSeekers.com,* etc., and of course, major franchise sites as well.

Feature Your Company's Special Services and Statistics

Use screens that highlight special services your company offers, including the number of agents, market share, and ancillary services. If your large franchise offers warranty programs or concierge services, this is a great place to profile this information. Smaller companies may list more personal and local services that would interest a homeowner. Include referral networks and mortgage services as well if they are available.

Feature Your Personal Web Presence

Use several screens to feature the diversity of your Web site. If your site is designed to offer convenient links to often-used information sites, demonstrate these value-added services in your presentation. Take screen captures of the home pages of the most important links. Sites can include local community information, statistics, park and recreation information, etc. A seller will be interested in knowing that your personal Web portal can offer immediate information so conveniently and easily.

Scan Samples of Your Special Reports

Demonstrate your communication and reporting services. Include the type of reports the seller can expect to receive. Examples are "Top Producer® Marketing Summary" reports, Agent2000® reports, and so forth. Scan in a sample report and perhaps have a hard copy to demonstrate what the report looks like. Its contents will give the homeowner the opportunity to be comfortable and clear about your plans to communicate activity and status.

By showing copies of these software reports you will commit to keeping the seller highly informed as to the progress and process of marketing the home. Some Web sites offer Web-based communication allowing your clients and customers to access a part of your Web site to obtain information regarding status and feedback. Copy and include this format in your presentation to help the seller visualize what reports will be provided by you on a regular basis.

Show Off Your Site Tracking

If your Web site has been designed to include tracking software, this is the perfect opportunity to demonstrate how you actually use site management for identifying activity. It is here you can delineate what pages get the most sessions and how you streamline and tailor your marketing efforts to procure the most exposure. This assures the seller that you are in command of what advertising investments work for you, and that you have the history to prove it. Having this information can often eliminate the seller "demanding" where the property will be advertised. It also is proof positive that there are those media that have historically generated more responses. Finally, correlate your surges in activity with specific ads, direct mail programs, or media advertisements that "drove" activity to your Web site.

Demonstrate the Power of Your Electronic Communication Tools

If you are using software communication tools such as auto responders, ask the homeowner to get involved in writing the "automatic report" that will feature information about this property. The auto responder acts as a type of "fax on demand" response to information requests through e-mail. There are many ways to use the auto responder, but a sure way to close on a listing interview is to get the seller's help in writing the details for this response. Include this value-added service in your digital listing presentation. (For more on auto responders, see Chapter 4).

Demonstrate the Power of Your E-Newsletters

If you are using a mail list to communicate with your different databases, share this information with your prospective seller. Indicate in your presentation how this Web communication tool is used as a lead generator. By taking a screen capture or copy of your electronic newsletter you can demonstrate to the seller how your personal digital mail lists give you the opportunity to contact interested parties at any time with new and changing information about properties, with one easy e-mail message.

Take the Seller on a Virtual Tour!

Virtual tours are another great item to display in your presentation. Offer the seller a "hands-on" visual of what an online tour of this home will look like. The virtual tour is the "presell" of a property for interested buyers; they can "stroll" through the property online, in the comfort of their own homes, prior to actually making an appointment to see the home. You can save a tour on a disc and demonstrate the tour without being online. The seller may not be familiar with this new program, and it might just get you the listing. Show how an e-gallery (a stack of discs personalized with your photo and company logo) acts as an enticement for prospective buyers viewing the home. The discs also can serve as "live" tours for other prospective buyers or their agents to promote the property.

Show the Seller "Where to Go"

Offer information about the latest sites, such as *Improvenet.com* and *MarthaStewart.com,* that provide ideas for repairs and decorating, and other sites for local contractor information.

Keep the Seller Connected

If your Web site offers back-end services, train the seller on how to access 24-hour marketing updates and progress reports on this property. Demonstrate how activity reports and even brochures can be downloaded and viewed by the homeowner at any time, keeping the seller closely connected to you and your consistent marketing efforts.

Electronic Key Boxes

The newest addition to electronic services is the use of an electronic key box. SUPRA® has integrated the convenience of a Palm Pilot and an electronic key to help the agent stay connected with the activity on a particular property, without having to actually go to the property to download the showing activity.

The news is this is a terrific opportunity to "sell" the seller on how up-to-the-minute you are on the latest technology applications; you are on top of all facets of the selling process with the info right in the "palm" of your hand (no pun intended ;-)).

If the homeowner has concerns about security, explaining the use of the electronic key box (if it is used in your area) can mitigate that concern. Meet the seller's concerns about restricting the hours the home is available for showing with this new tool.

Using *e*KEY, agents can program the key box conveniently, on site. (More about SUPRA's electronic key boxes and their new *e*KEY in Chapter 9.)

The Wrap

All these "tools" are just a few of the latest innovations making the home buying and selling process easier for all the parties involved, especially the agent out there in the field!

You are presented with a golden opportunity to provide the latest information to your clients and customers and inform them of these new tools and service opportunities. By incorporating these tools into your listing presentation, you demonstrate your commitment to providing cutting edge applications, products, and services if the seller lists with you. For the newly discriminating consumer, your sophisticated knowledge provides them the comfort and confidence that you are the right choice—while making your job easier, more organized, and most definitely saving you time and money!

*T*ech *T*ips

*C*heck out the latest in virtual assistant and phone follow-up paging systems. Instead of giving your sellers a ton of phone numbers, begin looking at a way to offer a one-number system. It's easier, faster, and much more professional. Some major phone companies offer packages that are very affordable!

You might want to consider using both printed and electronic communications to engage the seller. Print copies of your electronic listing presentation and offer to give a copy to the homeowner for future reference after you get the job.

If you offer the seller video "training" tapes, don't forget to get them back and put them back into your inventory.

Design your presentation to be interesting and educational as you walk the prospect through the latest objectives, opportunities, and special aspects of your service. The digital presentation is designed to be used over and over again, simply by changing the opening frames with the names, addresses, and photos of the subject property. It's easy! It's also a fun way to present our business with the customized program to help win the job!

Remember too, however, that not every seller is ready for the "electronic" show. *Always customize your presentations to fit your market and clientele.*

Chapter 9

Cool Stuff You Should Know

The more you get involved with the vast electronic universe out there, the more you will figure out that it's a full-time job just to keep up with it!

Too much information is just as bad as having no information! Therein lies the value of the future super agent for any business: becoming the "Knowledge and Information Center" for your customer and client base.

We all value time as our most precious commodity. It is strictly a "human" construction we are obsessed with! However, since we measure our very lives with it, "saving" time has become a most prized goal.

We can all cut our own grass and change the oil in our cars, but that doesn't mean we want to! With the overabundance of information, and the constant upgrading of technology, communications, and their respective applications, the value of the 21st century service provider will be in helping people get the information they need, when they need it, from a central place. Hopefully, you will position yourself to be one of the sources for that information.

Getting the information out will take digital transmissions, printed transmissions, and the personal touch. This chapter is devoted to some of the latest places to get new ideas and time-savers you will need to keep yourself connected and your clients and customers up to date. So, here are a few ideas to help you keep up with the latest new tools, gadgets, and great places to get information.

Saving Time for YOU!

Just like you need to be "information central" for your clients and customers, you need the same services for yourself! How do you keep your focus with the whirl of information, new service demands, and the constant acceleration of new tools?

Start with a Plan

In Chapter 10 we talk about life balance and how important planning is to determine if you are heading where you want to end up. One of the best books to help you implement a plan step-by-step is Tom Gegax's new book *Winning in the Game of Life*. Tom talks about being the CEO and coach for yourself and how you define the steps necessary to get where you want to go. For a different kind of winning that isn't just about money and material success, learn from Tom how winning through a unified approach, prioritizing, strategies, and life mission can change the way you live your life and get you the life you really want.

Coaching Is the Key

Tom Gegax talks about personal coaching and how sometimes we might need outside help. A smart way to keep your focus for both personal and professional productivity is to engage someone to help you through professional "coaching."

There are many different types of coaches out there eager to guide you to a higher success level. Decide if you are looking for production coaching to increase your volume or personal life balance coaching to seek a more peaceful and enriched lifestyle. Perhaps your plan will call for more focus on your finances where a different type of coaching would be appropriate.

Be sure to engage a coaching service that shares *your* idea of success and where you personally want to go. There are coaches who will call you on a regular basis to "drill" you on production commitments and other career-oriented issues. For yourself, decide on what type of full "coaching and training" best suits you.

Choose a coaching company that specializes in the real estate field and can help you in the following aspects of your personal success model:

- Personal development
- Technology and Internet training
- Real estate sales/investment
- Network marketing
- Small business/home business
- Franchise launching and business planning

I recently worked with a group from Draper, Utah; the team that provides coaching to the Automation Quest Programs. If you are interested in more information go to *http://www.Coaching-Institute.com*.

The Full Solution

One of the important aspects of getting with the 21st century business model is the issue of buying the right hardware and software and having it configured just right for you. Look for a business that provides a full technology solution to your needs. This includes guidance on buying hardware, software, financing, and most importantly, ongoing training and support. Anyone can sell you products, whether they are Web sites or hardware; the key is in the ongoing support after the sale! This is especially true when you purchase a Web template. Ask the right questions to get the answers you need before investing your hard-earned money in the wrong or incomplete tools. Check out *http://www.AutomationQuest.com*, an interesting site to use as a comparison to other competitors for technology solutions. An important aspect is the ongoing coaching and tech support!

Moving On Up

Well, you've come this far, and now you know there is more you need to know. A great solution to keeping up and moving up the ladder of Internet applications to our daily business is Michael Russer's new book/workshop/training called *e-POWER: Online Success Strategies for Real Estate Professionals.* Twice the size of his former workbook, "Mr. Internet" has pushed the envelope even further to help us get fully suited up for this digital stuff. Michael's approach to the Internet and its many uses is detailed, comprehensive, and easily accessible. For more information go to *http://www.ePowerWorks.com*.

Getting Certified Before Being Certifiable

"e-Pro" is a new Internet professional certification series offered through the National Association of REALTORS®. For more information go to *http://www.eProInfo.com*. Here's what One Realtor Place had to say about the new upcoming program:

> e-Pro is the new certification developed by the National Association of REALTORS® and its technology education partner *Websuite.com* with the assistance of Michael Russer, Internet expert, and formerly Dr. Barbara Hoffmann, Instructional Developer/Top Producing Realtor. e-Pro is not a "technology" certification but rather an "Internet Profes-

sional" certification. Agents with the e-Pro certification will demonstrate to the online buying and selling consumer that they are Internet-enabled and trained to help serve clients and customers in the online world of real estate transactions.

More Great Links for Training and Information

There are billions more places to learn. Following is a quick list of places to find information about online courses, training, schedules for upcoming seminars, and sources for information:

Allen Hainge Seminars	www.afhseminars.com
Women's Council of Realtors	www.WCR.org
Residential Sales Council	www.rscouncil.com
One Realtor Place	www.OneRealtorPlace.com
e-Power! Newsletter	mailto: join-ePower_news@lists.epowernews.com
Real Estate Professional	www.TheRealEstatePro.com
Mr. Internet's Site	www.russer.com

Neat Links to Help You

The problem with printed materials is that just about the time the ink is dry the information changes. We've included a list of neat links that are available for you to help your clients and customers with their needs. There are thousands and thousands of Web sites selling everything for the home and the property transaction. Here are a few that have proved to be valuable in helping me help the customer:

Decorating and Home Improvement	www.ImproveNet.com
Translation Sites for E-mail	www.t-mail.com
Computer Training Online	www.DPEC.com
Veterans Administration Loans	www.VALoans.com

Daily Updates

To keep abreast of the ever-changing world of real estate, get your info in easy, quick, "byte-sized" pieces that get to the point fast. You can scan the highlights to keep aware of nuances. Here are four sites that will help you do just that:

Inman News	*www.Inman.com*
Realty Times	*www.RealtyTimes.com*
Real Estate Data	*www.MonsterData.com*
The Industry Standard	*www.TheStandard.com*

Follow the new "Cyberstar" strategies and tips that work on Allen Hainge's Web site that include training, hot tips, and real time application to the integration of real estate and technology. To learn more about how real estate agents are using the new tech tools to do more business with profit, check out Allen Hainge's Cyberstar Newsletter at *www.afhseminars.com* (e-mail to *news@afhseminars.com*).

The Personal Digital Assistant (PDA)

The pocket answer to being electronically connected is the ever-popular Palm Pilot Personal Digital Assistant. This computerized, handheld device stores and updates personal schedules, calendars, addresses, and memos. It can also retrieve e-mail from your PC for viewing when convenient for you. It is a fast-growing technology, and Palm, Inc., in California, is the leading provider at this time. The PDA replaces hauling around those big, cumbersome personal organizers loaded with those itty-bitty pieces of paper that inevitably get lost the moment we really need them.

The PDA Made for Real Estate

A Personal Digital Assistant (PDA) by itself can only perform as a contact management tool, unless it is tied to a network that offers expanded services, such as your local MLS. With our offices becoming more "virtual" every day, the agent of today requires versatility and information away from the office or desktop. Having the MLS inventory updated daily in the "palm of your hand" could be a great timesaver.

The SUPRA® company recognized this early. SUPRA married the convenience of the PDA to a network that makes the agent a greater "information center," leveraging technology to save time, lower costs, and provide upgraded services to the client and customer. SUPRA combined the information and convenience of a Palm Pilot with the electronic key box in an "easy-to-have-with-you-always" tool. This combination, referred to as the SUPRA® *e*KEY, offers several conveniences:

- Log of activity at your listings
- Multiple listing updates
- Status on your personal listings
- Buyer profiles
- Hot Sheets on command
- Daily messages
- House member roster updates

This streamlining of communications offers you the ability to send information to all kinds of people on a regular basis. It's all about a new level of service delivered via an automated system with consistency and value-added information. This fills a great need for the active agent who has always had the challenge of being the information provider to myriad clients and customers in different decision and action levels pertaining to their individual personal real estate needs. This tool helps us keep "connected" to our business and fills our desire to be personally productive and valuable to the transaction.

SUPRA's *e*KEY is available with a Top Producer® Contact Manager software made expressly for the Palm Pilot, allowing a more convenient and timely way to keep customer communications organized and available, while also maintaining great records!

If you are willing to learn how to do more effective work from your digital office (while watching your kids play ball) look into the latest innovations with the *eKEY* PDA from SUPRA. For more info, go to *www.suprakey.com*.

Million Dollar Ads That Work

It is pretty apparent that doing the same things yields the same results. If you poll agents across the country, you will find that only the top producers have changed the overused, tired, print advertising copy. Most of us still cling to the old ways when writing ads, flyers, and brochures to market ourselves, our companies, and our inventory.

The best book I've come across on this topic is marketing guru Diane Armitage's *Million Dollar Ads*. This dynamo is the brilliant marketer and business consultant behind the big names and national companies you know in our industry. She understands the basics of effective direct response marketing.

According to Armitage, your advertising has to change to evoke response. The new millennium demands a distinction in services and your attention to how your advertising dollars are spent. Instead of outspending your competition, Diane advises that implementing direct response marketing can decrease your expenditures 45 percent and increase business over 36 percent, as it has for those top people who benefit from her expertise.

Diane now consults and guides us through the easy science of direct response marketing and how it serves the client and customer with results and not just features. If you plan on growing your business to a new level and you are willing to spend the time to learn about technology, to buy the hardware and software necessary, and are willing to become knowledgeable about the Internet and the communication tools necessary to be connected, then take the time to learn about how to create million dollar ads, flyers, mailers, Web site features, and even e-mail blasts and letters that actually *work*. For more information, go to *www.WriteBrain.com* where you can e-mail Diane directly.

Books That Help!

There is so much information coming at you daily that it is hard to prioritize where to direct your attention first. I've listed below a few of the books that have helped me to really understand the impact of change on our new industry. Check out just a few to help you get the full scoop on how to understand and adapt the changes we are challenged with today.

Sarah Ban Breathnach, *Simple Abundance*

Dr. Stephen Covey, *First Things First*

Dr. Stephen Covey, *The 7 Habits of Highly Effective People*

Danny "Fabulous" Cox, *There Are No Limits*

Blanche Evans, *The Hottest e-Careers in Real Estate*

Tom Gegax, *Winning in the Game of Life*

Michael Gerber, *The E-Myth Revisited*

Seth Godin, *Permission Marketing*

Guy Kawasaki, *Rules for Revolutionaries*

Viki King, *Beyond Visualization*

Orison Swett Marden, *Every Man a King*

Andrew Matthews, *Being Happy*

W. Mitchell, *It's Not What Happens to You, It's What You Do About It*

Price Pritchett, Ph.D., *Quantum Leap Strategy*

Price Pritchett, Ph.D., *You^2*

Anthony Robbins, *Awaken the Giant Within*

Anthony Robbins, *Unlimited Power*

Barbara Sher, *Wishcraft*

Andrea Stoddard, *Living a Beautiful Life*

John Tuccillo, *Click & Close: E-Nabling the Real Estate Transaction*

John Tuccillo, *The Eight New Rules of Real Estate*

Michael Vance/Deacon, *Think Out of the Box*

Buddy West and John Tuccillo, *Targeting the Over 55 Client*

Harold Wright, *How to Make 1,000 Mistakes in Business and Still Succeed*

Chapter 10

e-Prosper & Live Longer: Life Balance and 21st Century Real Estate

The third millennium brings with it a host of brand new opportunities, conveniences, and challenges. Have you noticed that the general pace of your life seems much quicker than it seemed just a few short years ago?

We were all led to believe that this technology stuff would automate systems and streamline our lives so that we had more time . . . and so, who has more time? Although we love the way technology is helping us move at the speed of light, we are not seeing our day-to-day lives slow down . . . yet. The learning curve does take a commitment to some up-front time and a willingness to integrate new things until they become reflexive and routine. Ultimately, the rewards of synergyzing, streamlining, and single processing will make details and systems easier to handle. It worked for washing machines; remember grandma's wringer washer? Now, we can just push a button and the magic of clean clothes happens. So hang in there. ;-)

Here's the real deal. I'll bet there will never be enough time to be, or to do, all that we think we would like to. It's not like time is a commodity that is available only to the Donald Trumps or the Michael Jordans of the universe. We all get the same equal measurement of time in a day in which we try to accomplish those things that create "our lives."

For the sake of self-esteem, health, and a stab at life balance, let's look at a few of the possibilities that can make the new millennium more satisfying, less guilt-ridden, and more fulfilling than the previous year . . . and this time for *real*.

Refocus

Take an honest look at yourself and your life. Sometimes this can be a bit painful if you happen to be in judgment mode instead of objectivity. The goal here is to refocus on the new plan and create the life you want, have always wanted, or were at some point afraid to allow yourself. Proceed boldly and be as honest with yourself as possible.

The questions are basic and simple. How about a reality check?

- Are you living the life you always envisioned?
- Do you have a child-like anticipation for getting up every morning and embracing the day?
- Do you lust for the adventure and challenges you are exposed to daily?
- Do you see the miracles that happen in your life . . . and appreciate them?
- Do you really "live" the moment, or is your day a blur of "should-haves"?
- Do you realize that your life is controlled by your decisions and choices when opportunities present themselves?

Many of us are too doggone busy to "seize the day," and as a result we let life control us. It's not unusual, just unfortunate and all too common. We get taken in by the "To Do List" instead of the "I Want List" of life.

I am not suggesting that we abandon responsibility and become hedonistically selfish, but there is a happy medium here of enjoying what we have, while we have it, and creating more satisfaction, comfort, and joy as we live this adventure we call "life."

Each of us has the same 24 hours every day to "write the script" of our life. Some of us allow others to write it for us. We then have an excuse to spend the rest of our lives feeling frustrated and victimized, creating disease in ourselves and those around us. Not a good plan. This is a recipe for not living well. Why do we allow these things to happen to us? Here are some guidelines to help us create a richer, more satisfying life adventure.

Get Out of Judgment and Into Curiosity

For the moment, try not to judge. Get curious and notice how you have been living your life for the past few years. If you can create it, then you can change it. If you are skeptical about this power, try going back to whining and complaining and see how much better things don't get! Move aside for those of us who are sick and tired of being sick and tired. It's not age, or hormones, or money, or opportunity that hold us back. Quite simply, it is ourselves.

Take Responsibility

Look around. You are the result of thoughts you created and acted upon before. No? Well, look in the mirror for a minute. Hair long or short? Some moment in time the style, color, and length of your hair was your choice. Body weight healthy or unhealthy? Were you savagely force fed to gain that ten pounds or more, or did you do it yourself, one bite at a time? Credit card balances too high? Were you hijacked by a crazed shopper and forced to overspend at your favorite department store, or were the selections made and charged by you?

You are the living composite of your own thoughts and actions. You are fully responsible for how you think, what you choose to focus on, and how you talk to yourself. Even if you say you are not responsible, you still made the decision to allow someone else to dictate the look and feel of your life.

Life Tip

You have the power to create and design your life.

The weak begin by offering excuses for whatever they lack. They blame their childhoods, or physical problems, or bad breaks. But you can't snow yourself. Deep down you know that you have the power to change your world. For the moment, let's just say you are somewhat "disconnected" and are taking this opportunity to reconnect.

Think back to a time you felt "unstoppable"; truly focused on what you really wanted. Was it having children? Owning a home? Getting your license? Starting a business? Marrying the love of your life? What was the difference? You are the same person now, but then you had a different focus, a different "attention" factor, a different energy behind your motivation. Find that energy again and apply it to what you would love to change about your life, starting right now.

There are situations, scenarios, and "Murphyisms" that are ready to derail your plan. So what? You may have to detour, bob, weave, run, jump, switch gears, and get up and start all over again until you find another way to have what you so richly deserve from yourself. The choice is clearly yours when you keep your eyes on what you want.

- If you want health, give it to yourself in ways you know produce health.

- If you want love, love yourself first and the rest will come.
- If you want financial success, give yourself the opportunity to allow it to come to you through the planning and fruits of your labor and attention.
- If you want "you," take the responsibility to give to yourself first.

Sounds too easy? Maybe at first. When you become fascinated with something, such as learning another language, or gourmet cooking, or playing golf or tennis, you become better at it and more knowledgeable after investing your time and attention. The same applies here. There is a requirement, however. You must give it the time and pure attention to create it, nurture it, fantasize about it, and allow it into your life. Don't believe me . . . just try it and let me know how you are doing.

You take the responsibility to decide what you want, when you want it, and that you can in fact have it, whatever "it" is. You've got plenty of help *after* you make the commitment to yourself.

Choose Your Big Rocks: "The Big Rock Theory"

Dr. Stephen Covey, in his book *The 7 Habits of Highly Effective People,* quotes a story of a professor teaching a class about the placement of rocks in a glass container. It is eminently easier to place big rocks into the container first, followed by little rocks, sand, and finally water, than it is to reverse the process. When designing your life, decide what your "big rocks" are, and schedule them as designated time slots or days in your annual calendar. Accomplish this by beginning with the end in mind. Then work backwards from the end of the upcoming calendar year.

Simply block out the days of the year that you have marked with your top priorities, or "big rocks." The process will take some personal searching as to what you give high priority to these days. Blocking out priority days for those important things in life minimizes the possibilities of the "no-time-for-it" excuse.

Plug in the Days for Specific Events

This is the place to schedule all those many things that you have grumbled that you never had time for. Take this opportunity to pencil in those things that you want to add to your life. It could be a quarterly "meet a good friend for lunch" day. Include one day a month for personal grooming and doctor's visits. Don't overlook a regular, quarterly "self-improvement" day for special seminars or courses you have been meaning to attend. Ideas to think about are learning a new language, art lessons, gourmet cooking classes, or joining a wine tasting club.

Schedule a "Date Night"

Your personal relationships will benefit greatly by choosing a regular weekly "date night" to spend with your significant other. According to Dr. Wayne Prepura, a relationship specialist from the Chicago area, statistics show that it takes a minimum of two-and-one-half quality hours a week of face-to-face time to keep a relationship nurtured. Just a little over 21 minutes of real, sincere, connected time per day can help ensure a rich and rewarding relationship that survives the ups and downs of life with one of the best gifts life offers: a partner or friend. This "special" time also reaffirms that there are important cornerstones in your life that have priority. Those times and special people can keep you on track while letting your loved ones know they are important to you.

Plan Family Nights

Sadly in our society, the family sitting around the dinner table at the end of the day is a rarity. It is a different time that we live in; doing the "family dinner thing" every night like Ozzie and Harriet is not always possible. However, planning "family nights" can keep a family communicating and growing together. Take a few nights a week that work around football practice, music lessons, etc., and have dinner or just time together. This is a great time to discuss vacation plans, educational days for museum trips, or special interest days for the whole family. Get everyone involved in the family "goal setting plans" that include meeting the financial obligations to afford the "goodies." When the whole family understands the big picture, you create a solid foundation for a strong and meaningful family unit built on mutual respect, understanding, and love.

For an interesting look at how we process time and our time perceptions for living in the moment, check out Joseph Bailey and Richard Carlson's book *Slowing Down to the Speed of Life*. They have an interesting theory on "manipulating the perception of time, especially with young family and creative experiences." We need to learn how to have more quality time with the family, as opposed to just shoving everyone together and hoping to build bonds of trust and positive feelings.

Reserve a Quarterly "Chill Out" Day for Yourself

If Edison, Ford, Firestone, Carrel, and Lindberg allowed for creative time, so can you. In James Newton's book *Uncommon Friends*, Jim talks about how the big five were diligent about quiet and creative time and allowed daily time to just "be" and think. In our fast-paced world, this seems to be a luxury but it is really a necessity for us all. It is much easier to hide in "busyness" than to courageously ponder our challenges for the solution that is waiting to be discovered.

Decide ahead of time what you would like to do with yourself on that special day. Sarah Ban Breathnach, in her book *Simple Abundance*, relays the importance of "downtime" and encourages quiet activities. If you enjoy antiques, take an afternoon and stroll through a few stores you've passed by. You'll be less frazzled and of more value when you're back in the trenches.

If You Break Your Body, Where Will You Live?

We can't seem to get in our daily 30 minutes of exercise, and yet we succumb to hauling around an extra 10 to 20 pounds every minute we are alive, draining our energy and impairing optimum proficiency. Make a pact with yourself that from this point forward, "I choose to be healthy and fit for the rest of my life." As we get older, the body seems less forgiving, and health is not a commodity that we can take for granted any longer. This requires a life change that may seem quite uncomfortable at first. We aren't always crazy about changing our personal habits. The first couple of times it might be rough, but you'll begin looking forward to that daily walk or an evening racquetball game. It's your life, and you've got the pen in hand to change the script.

Plan Out Vacation Days

If the president of the United States can have a vacation, so can you. Block out days and dates to work around as you begin filling your calendar with activities. Consider a quarterly three-day weekend away to refocus and refuel yourself, in addition to a couple weeks off when it suits you. Many of the top producers of our industry have learned the value of quiet time, reevaluation time, and reenergizing time to meet the new demands of customers, clients, and just plain life! This may require that you develop a relationship with a fellow agent to cover for you (and you for them) when you need the breaks.

Control the Only Thing You Can

Did you ever notice that the people we envy the most are those individuals who seem to have it all? They never seem to have a bad hair day, their cars are immaculate, and their homes are well-appointed, rich in character, interesting, and comfortable. In addition, they seem to have limitless energy and a great attitude to match.

If you are like most of us, you either wish you knew their secret or you write them off as not being "real." The truth is they are loaded with integrity and self-esteem because they have taken control of themselves first, and then are much more able to roll with the punches that life throws their way. It just makes sense to control ourselves, and not the world around us. Instead of being envious of those "together" types, give yourself permission to enjoy those things you would like to have in your life. It's a lot like shopping; if you see something that you like about someone else, their life, their business, it is available to you and not reserved for only a special few.

Get Tough—What Is Your Time Worth?

When you are new in the real estate business, you are willing to list a doghouse if you think you can sell it. And you will put up with the cantankerous, miserable, unfriendly people who live there. After 21 years in the business, here is what I've learned (albeit later than I would have preferred):

There are just some people you cannot make happy.

Think about how precious your time is. You are not going to be the perfect salesperson for every person on earth. Listen to your "gut" and pay attention. If the situation feels right, go for it. If that little voice in your head has you hesitating, or you're doing a great sales job on your head to avoid that voice, back off. You decide if the exchange for your time, energy and *life* "time" is worth your compensation. Dealing with the negatives may be easier because you've made the choice consciously.

It shouldn't take a brush with near catastrophe to make you realize this life thing is a short-time stint and every second of every minute counts. Somehow we get lost in the maze of "doing" instead of "being" and fritter away hours doing things we don't want to do with people and activities we don't want to be involved with. It makes us frustrated, cranky, and not pleasant to be around.

When you allow someone to waste your time *it's your fault*. If you work with people you don't like or don't feel right about, *it's your choice. It's your life you are spending*. There is a station at the end of this ride. The winner is the one who enjoyed the ride and learned from every moment how to be a better person and helped others become better as well.

Do It, Delegate It, or Dump It

If you have a pile of old magazines you've been meaning to read, then read them or dump them. If you have an overpriced listing that drains you of time, money, and energy, then get a price reduction or send the seller on his or her way. If you hate bookkeeping, then get a bookkeeper. The idea is to deal with "whatever it is" and not procrastinate. Examine why you are not addressing the issue, figure it out, then move on.

Delete, Delete, Delete

There is power in simplicity. Start simplifying everything—closets, basements, office drawers, paper work—you'll feel like you've lost ten pounds and have lots more energy. If you can't use it—whatever it is—pass it on to someone who can.

You also need to delete the toxic people in your life. Sometimes this is tough to do, especially if they are in your family. Decide in your heart of hearts that no one can "contaminate" your space with negativity or bad vibes unless you give them permission to do so. Give your attention and time to those people who compliment your energy. Seek out those special individuals who are contributing and positive people. If you succumb to the constant depletion of those eternally needy individuals who take but never give, well then, you guessed it, it's your choice.

Forgive You, Forgive Them

Forgiving can be challenging, particularly if you are "Italian" at heart. (Just kidding, but the Italian kids know what I am talking about. ;-)) It takes a ton more energy to carry a grudge than it does to learn from the experience, forgive yourself, and move on. Energy is a real commodity. If you squander it, or use it unwisely, you are depleting your own resources.

There are plenty of situations and people that can make you crazy, angry, disappointed, and downright hurt. The truth is, we are all human. We make mistakes. Every one of us at one time or another wishes we could take back moments, even seconds, in time to "live over" and do the right thing; the thing we really intended to do with our hearts. There is, unfortunately, no rewind button on life.

Rarely does someone lament, "I would love to live that moment over again, just so I can mess up a little bit more than I did the first time." Usually, when tempers subside and the air clears, arguments are seen as dumb to begin with, but with pride and saving face at stake, the war continues.

The first step is to forgive yourself, but for many of us this seems to be the toughest thing to do. Did you ever notice how brutally you talk to yourself? Ever lose your keys? Forget something you needed? Lose an "important" piece of paper? The manner in which we address ourselves is sad; we would never think of speaking to a friend the way we reprimand ourselves. Cut yourself a break and move on. After all, most times our "mistake" is not a world wide event. ;-)

It's impossible for us to be compassionate to others when we whale on ourselves. Lighten up and be sensible. It is rarely a life or death situation, so laugh at yourself and chill. There are plenty of people who are willing to do a job on you, so you don't need to be the first in line.

Go about your life in forgiveness. That doesn't mean you need to allow the same situations to hurt you or your loved ones over and over again. It just means that to harbor ill feelings may make *you* ill. It's not worth it. At the final closing, the only thing that matters is how *you* lived *your* life, and not how dopey someone else was to you. Learn, move on, and be grateful for your blessings and "learning" experiences. There is always a solution. There is always a way out.

Get Real

Although it seems otherwise, no one has the "perfect" life all the time. Even Cindy Crawford has had a bad hair day (I'd personally love to see it ;-)) and Bill Gates certainly has had his challenges. If money were the answer, some people who were quite wealthy but hugely unhappy, would still be around to enjoy this life today. Life is a learning game. The winner is enriched with experience, empowered to live life to its fullest, and gives back whenever and wherever possible.

Life is happening in the moments you breathe in and out. Not just when the kids are at school, not just when the holidays are over, but also right now as you read this. The future is planned from the future, not the present, because the present is too late. A diamond becomes more valuable in the time and pressure of becoming the luminous jewel that it is, not only after it is cut and polished to perfection. You and I are a lot like that rough diamond. Life's impacts can polish us to perfection, or we can allow the pressure and the cuts to destroy us.

There is no fairness chip in the poker game of life. Everybody gets dealt cards. The game is played by choices and decisions that we make, and we have the power to change in a moment.

Picture the buttons on the radio in your car. If you don't like the song on the first station, there are plenty of buttons to push to select a new frequency. The higher the frequency in life, the richer the songs.

Are you proud of the challenges that made you shine? Did the tough lessons or tough love make you better at loving? Did the harsh lessons about trust make you wiser, brighter, with a secure wisdom that draws people to you for guidance? Does the hero within you glow with the confidence and poise you garnered from the challenges you've overcome?

My friend W. Mitchell has had his share of challenges. In his book *It's Not What Happens to You, It's What You Do About It,* Mitchell relates how two tragic accidents caused him to be brutally burned and now physically handicapped. He explains how his scarred face, fingerless paws, and the genuine happiness in his heart are used as a mental image of the power of the human mind to transcend circumstances. Here's what we learn from Mitchell:

> Nothing, absolutely nothing is absolute. Your life is entirely what you decide it is. It is your spaceship, your up, your down. The Universe starts in your head and spreads out into the world. Change what happens in your head and the Universe changes. Really.

Mitchell's spirit continues to be an inspiration to me. Whenever you feel sorry for yourself, give him a call.

Gratitude (Grazie, Grazie, Grazie!)

You may not share my feelings about this, but you might think about it. I truly believe that Americans are the luckiest people on the planet. We are privileged to live in America, the finest country in the world. We are so casual about our freedom, expectant of abundance, demanding of those who serve us, and somewhat oblivious to the many gifts around us.

I, however, have learned the hard way to be very, very grateful for all of my blessings. When I am whiney and in self-pity Mitchell helps me focus on my "haves" and not my "have-nots." My gift is that every morning when I wake, I enjoy the comfortable and easy use of my body to move around freely and at will. I am truly blessed that I wake up in a warm and comfortable bed. I open my eyes and clearly see colors and objects. I hear the music of life as it begins to hum all around me. I awake in a country that is not at war or oppressing its citizens. In almost every nook and cranny of this great country is the great opportunity to fulfill every desire that life offers. I know that there is food in the kitchen, warm water in the bathroom, and I am a very blessed person.

We forget the luxuries we are given. We "compare" ourselves to the megastars, the megapersonalities, those with more money, attention, looks, lucky breaks, etc., and focus on what we don't have, rather than on the huge abundance of gifts that we do have.

We need to focus more on our wants, and not give attention to what we don't want. The laws of attraction are universal. You attract what you think about the most, what you direct your energy to. So it's impossible to attract success if you focus on your failures. We are unable to attract love if we don't love ourselves. We can't attract health when we focus on our illnesses and disease. Do a focus check several times a day. When you begin to feel uneasy, notice where you are focused.

The Wrap

- Change your focus, change your life.
- Be grateful for all your gifts everyday, several times a day.
- Be open to the abundance of good and positive things.
- Know that all of your actions have reactions.
- You create the power in your life.
- Forgive yourself, forgive others, but be smart about it.
- Take your power back. No one wants to hang with a "whiner."
- Live life. Live it on purpose. When you hold the person you care about, hold them like it's the last time you'll ever touch them. Feel the magnificence of life fully in that moment. Make your action in the moment count in a positive, empowering way. Life will be richer, you will notice more, be more appreciative of life. You will be more interesting,

quietly in control of yourself, wiser, and more attractive to those around you who feel your serenity and want to share that stability.
- Be in the vicinity of "greatness." It rubs off and makes those around it great too. If you choose to "rub shoulders," rub with someone who can teach you, so you can teach others.
- In this very moment, call someone you love and *tell them*. Don't be shy. Let them know you are "crazy" about them, and that they enrich your life just by being them and you are a better person because of them. Jump on the moment in time when you can tell them, show them. When you are with those special people, touch them like it's the last time you can hug them and feel them close to you. Someday you will miss that opportunity. Revel in the moment of connection. Your "significant other" may think you are crazy, or having an affair (just kidding). The idea here is that we put things like this off because we say, "They know I love them, I don't have to tell them or show them" WRONG! Every single human being longs for love, acceptance, and recognition. Make your moments in life count. Buy a single flower, tuck a yellow Post-it note where it can be found later, send an electronic greeting card . . . but *share what's in your heart*. The returns are enormous for you and for those you love.
- Finally—the toughest thing for some of us—let yourself accept the love and care of others in return.

Technology and Living Life in the 21st Century

As mentioned, life seems faster and more demanding every day. The miracle of technology, however, affords us an incredible opportunity for growth and "connection."

All the information that was ever available is now in one place. That "place" is wherever you are and can access the Internet. Communication is now impervious to borders, business hours, holidays, and high costs. We have access to a universe of information for the price of a local phone call. So how does this help you build your business, organize your life, and care for your family?

Just as the wringer washer has been replaced by a much more efficient model, so too have been the tools that we previously depended on. Just as we agree that life is moving at a much quicker pace, so too are the inevitable changes that accompany new plans, changed itineraries, and the constant moving of friends, family, clients, and customers.

Productivity Software

Use a personal productivity software package such Microsoft Outlook to organize and track the daily obligations and events of life. The address book can be sorted for holiday greetings, birthdays, important dates, follow-ups, and personal and professional information. No need to envy the friend that always remembers birthdays. Just enter birth dates in your personal productivity software and they will pop-up in plenty of time for you to send an "electronic" birthday card or the old fashioned kind that you mail.

Just because you have a digital schedule, doesn't mean that you must haul around your computer and "boot up" every time you want to check your schedule. Simply print your calendar for easy access during the course of your day.

It's All about Building Relationships

The ultimate power of the Internet is connecting people with people. How many times have you had a quick thought about a friend or colleague? You wonder if he or she is doing okay and you would love to say hello . . . if you only had the time. Well, e-mail makes it easy, convenient, fast, and loaded with value from the heart when you think of someone during your busy day and send a one-liner that says, "Hi. I'm thinking about you!"

The Internet will bring us together if we *choose* to be connected. Set aside a morning or a regular time to reconnect with friends, family, customers, clients, and show off your digital presence. If they are on e-mail, here is a script that works:

> Hi! Long time no connect! This is Terri Murphy and I am determined to keep those people who I (love, like, appreciate, want, need, etc.) in my life and connected online. I have a new e-mail address: *Terri@TerriMurphy.com*. I am building my new digital database and updating my records. Can you verify your birthday? Would you be interested in receiving my newsletter? I also from time to time offer some free reports. Would that be of interest?
>
> I am so glad to be connected again. It seems like we are always just too busy, but this will definitely help us stay connected. See you online!

It's so easy to do the small things. Drop a note, let someone you know that you care about them. Whether you are following up after a client move or checking up 30 days later, the new ticket to success is customer service and satisfaction. Staying connected is the key to organizing yourself to make it happen.

Planning Your Security

Clearly, we need to provide for ourselves in this material world. Food, shelter, and clothing cost money, and since many of us are sole providers, strictly dependent on our active efforts, financial planning is imperative and a smart thing to do. To keep our relevancy to the industry, we need to be very connected to what our expenses are and the return on our marketing efforts.

Tools to Help You

It is imperative that we begin to understand that we don't sell houses anymore, that the new real estate professional is selling services. Our marketing must be directed toward our new services, so we must be fully informed of what our expenses are and if the return on that investment is worth it.

There are many new ways to market ourselves; some of them are costly. Why would you continue to invest in an expense that showed little or no return?

Learn how to use tracking software to determine where your business is coming from. Begin to tailor the needs of your consumer, to position yourself and your services as continually valuable to your customers and clients.

The best place to begin is at the beginning. First, determine how much money you need to fulfill basic budgetary obligations such as mortgage/rent, food, utilities, insurance, medical, etc. Second, try to track your last two to three years of business expenses to determine what it cost you to generate the volume you have produced to date. At this point, you can begin to design a plan that will give you the freedom to live your life and earn income.

It doesn't have to be complicated, but begin with a simple sheet of paper or a page on your computer and make a list of what it is you want to accomplish in all areas of your business career. Entries that you may want to consider include the following:

- How much money do I need each month to pay my bills?
- How much do I want to earn each month?
- How much of that income will go to my tax account for paying income taxes?
- What percentage of my income will go directly to my retirement account?
- What kind of dollar allotment can I consider for investment purposes?
- What tools will I need to accomplish this?
- Do I have a budget for business expenses?
- Do I have an allotment for hardware and software?

- What are my goals for acquiring hardware and software that align with my financial budgets to increase business?
- What amount of savings reserve do I have to supplement the initial stages of securing and marketing listings until they close and generate cash flow?
- How many hours do I intend to work on prospecting per week?
- How many hours will I devote to servicing my present business?
- What amount of time will I designate to learning for continuing education, designations, and training?
- What personal program will I follow to contribute to learning, earning, and living a balanced life?

Consult a Pro

If you are unsure about how to set up your business plan, get a good small business counselor to help you determine what your short-term plan (six months) and your long-term plan (three to five years) will look like. Based on the economics in your area, you will be able to determine just how many listings and sales per month it will take to keep you solvent, make you comfortable for a while, or build you a wealth-producing system that can provide you with the life you want and a secure retirement.

Too many of us work like crazy, earn a lot of commissions, and end up with very little to live on. It is much easier today to track expenses through a software program such as Quicken than it was before. Focusing on what it costs to conduct business will help you to determine what promotional items or advertising expenses are worth your hard-earned dollars. There are lots of people out there willing to sell you tools, props, promotional items, gadgets, and toys that can "help" you sell more real estate. As your own "Head of Purchasing," you must determine if these are necessary, and, according to your very specific budget, cost-effective.

Define Your Marketing Plan

The next time someone calls saying that you have been selected as one of the first agents in your area to be invited to participate in a promotional advertising campaign by having your picture on the shopping carts at the local supermarket, you will be in a better position to determine if this fits into your overall advertising and promotional guidelines. It's your money. You should know what will be the best yield for the expenditure.

Plan Your Objectives and Goals

A business needs a good business plan to run efficiently. Unfortunately, we often don't have a clear idea of where we want to end up, how much it will cost to get there, or whether or not we can survive financially.

You are now the CEO and CFO of your own corporation. No one wants to run a company that has no plan to accumulate more business, no projections for dollars earned, and no retirement benefits available to the owner.

Develop and Plan an "Exit Strategy"

One of the primary reasons to begin building your digital database is to compete in 21st century currency: information. The value of your database is your gold mine! At some point you might be interested in leaving an area, leaving the business, or concentrating on a special area of the business. This change will require you to quantify your contacts in an electronic format; a database to sell, parlay, or use as a basis for selling your business.

A database provides you the freedom to sell your information at some point for some value. Nothing is absolute. Should you decide to get out of the real estate business, your broker, company, or a brand new agent might want to purchase your database and pay you a referral for a specific period of time. This is better than abandoning your life's work with no compensation.

Additionally, with the new tracking-and-matching powers of the Internet, your database information may have more value than you think down the line. In any case, you can't sell a stack of file boxes loaded with papers; your data must be digital, up-to-date, and viable.

Invest in Real Estate

Many of the top producers see value in property ownership. This is a great way to build a portfolio of life-supporting assets that give you the freedom to live life instead of working for a salary or commission. Since you already have the knowledge and the access to properties, think about buying at least one investment property per year. In ten years, at $100,000 a property, you are on your way to being a "millionaire." Smart property management and tenant selection, along with long- and short-term hold strategies, need to be determined to suit your life plan. Keep a couple of those great deals for yourself on an annual basis. Consult with your financial planner to map out a plan that can work for you.

The Wrap

Remember that power is knowing, and knowing where you are going and what you want to accomplish will help you focus and draw the energies and support you need to be successful at any business, especially real estate.

The only thing in the world that can be managed or controlled is *you*. Although there are many elaborate time management systems, digital or otherwise, the basic concept is that we can only manage ourselves. By having a plan to focus on as daily life kicks up the unexpected, you can move forward with those things that bring you what you really want out of this lifetime on a full and balanced scale.

Appendix A

Backing Up Data

When you work on your computer, you normally create and save your data on the hard drive itself. *Backing up* is the process by which you store critical data someplace *other than on the computer.* This is done for security reasons. If something—such as a flood, tornado, earthquake, or major power hit—affects the computer and wipes out the stored data, you still have access to the data because a backup copy was kept elsewhere.

What Should I Back Up?

The easy answer is anything you can't live without or that would take a long time to recreate. This includes databases, financial records, address books, and critical correspondence.

In general, you should make a complete backup of your system monthly. If not practical, you should make backups of every file that you cannot replace one way or another. If it would be costly for you to rekey it, back it up!

While software packages handle files differently, your key data files are generally in a few selected areas on a Windows machine: My Documents, My Files, and in the application folder if the application is unique or non-Microsoft. In addition to your data files, you should also back up your e-mail and contact files. Here are some specific places and files to look for:

- Eudora stores its e-mail and address book in .mbx files.
- Outlook Express lets you specify the location of its mail file, so it could be anywhere. Look for files named "mail," or your own name, to find your mail.
- Netscape Messenger defaults to "C:Program>Files> Netscape>Users>your name>Mail."
- Outlook 98 stores everything in a .pst file.
- Address books are usually in .pab files.
- Bookmarks. Netscape files this in: "C:Program>Files> Netscape>Users>yourname>bookmark.htm."
- Save your entire "C:Windows>Favorites" area.

Other files you may wish to save are *ini* files and your network and configuration settings.

How Do I Back Up?

Determine the software to be used for backing up. There are several software applications (commercial and shareware) that can automatically back up your data to whatever media you select. There is even software on your Windows machine that allows you to schedule backups when you want.

Set up your software and select the files that you want backed up. Each application is different, so check the instructions for the automatic backup schedule. If you are working on critical files, you may wish to manually store those to a Zip disk, diskette, or Superdisk after you have finished each day's work.

When Should I Back Up?

Early and often! Seriously, back up *before* your have the need to recover a file, and on a scheduled basis.

Suggested schedule for backups for a week are:

Day 1   entire hard drive
Days 2-7   files that changed on each day

When you get to Day 8, use a new set of disks or media for the complete backup. On Day 9, use the same disk that you used on Day 2. This helps to cycle the media and gives you the opportunity to recover data at specific points in time.

A complete monthly backup is good to have on hand. Two copies of your backups are better. Store one at your location and one off-site for the best possibility of recovery in case of disaster.

Which Media Should I Use?

Decide that your backup will be stored on removable media. Traditionally done on small floppy (1.44 MB) diskettes, the volume required to back up today's work would be overwhelming. In addition, diskettes are probably the least reliable way to manage your data. Your options today include tape, Zip disk, Superdisk (larger version of a floppy), tape, and R/W CDs (read/write CDs). Not all of these choices may be available to you depending on your system hardware.

Depending on what equipment you currently have or are willing to purchase, the following descriptions can help you determine which backup media is appropriate for you.

Zip Disk

Available in 100 MB and 250 MB sizes, Zip disks are fast, reliable, and your data is stored in the identical format you use it in.

A document file will be a document file and not a cryptic data file when stored to this media. It's portable as well. Hardware is around $100 and each disk is about $10. Zip disks are very popular which makes it easy to send files this way too.

SuperDisk

These 120 MB disks are similar to Zip disks, but not as popular. The hardware uses an internal bay of the computer and may be in combination with your A drive. SuperDisks look like floppy disks. They are fast, fairly reliable, and your data is stored in the identical format you use it in. A document file will be a document file and not a cryptic data file when stored to this media. It's portable as well. Hardware is around $150 and each disk is about $10-$12.

Tape

Tapes vary in capacity but can hold gigabytes of data. One liability to this storage medium is that is difficult to determine if files are stored correctly; usually files are stored in a condensed format. Files need to be "restored" in order to be accessible. Finally, reliability over time can diminish.

R/W CDs

This storage medium holds 650 MB of data. R/W CDs are not as fast as Zip disks or SuperDisks. It is a good choice for complete system backups or major applications. Large applications may be condensed to save space but smaller files can be written (burned) to the CD in the format that they are in. Hardware starts around $250 for an internal R/W CD drive. Disks can be purchased in quantity at $1.50 to $2.00 each.

Other Storage Options

If you don't wish to use disks, CDs, or tapes, you can opt to have your data backed up on the Internet. Several companies offer services that will back up your files whenever you are connected to the Internet. While not always practical for large files on a slow connection, this should be a serious consideration for anyone with ISDN, DSL, or T-1 connections. Search for "online backup" or "backup" in your favorite search engine to find companies that offer this service.

Appendix B

Sample e-Newsletters

E-Newsletter from Tupper Briggs

March 3, 2000
Real Estate Update
Tupper Briggs and The Mountain Home Team
RE/MAX Evergreen
Monthly Real Estate Market Report for Evergreen/Conifer, Colorado

The Economy
Not much new to report, but I always enjoy delivering good news, so I'll share some end-of-year stats that came in during February. Sales of existing homes set another record in 1999, for the 4th year in a row. Also, Colorado home values appreciated by an average of nearly 40% over the last 5 years, placing our state in the number two position (behind Michigan) in the nation.

Although the 2000 housing market promises to be robust, records are hard to break year-in and year-out. We expect this year to the third best year for real estate sales, behind 1998 and 1999. Probably best pictured as the other, downhill side of a high but gently-sloping mountain.

Real Estate News
If you haven't noticed the changes we're making in our marketing yet, watch for our new logo and team name, The Mountain Home Team. Our Realtor team now consists of me, John Henthorne, Jennifer Trinco, Dana Bossert and Peg Schroder. Our wonderfully supportive staff is made up of LeeAnn Marker, Office Mgr, Kim Hock, Listing Coordinator, Denise Morris, Closing Coordinator and Glenda Puyper, Ambassador of Goodwill (Call Coordinator). We're growing, but our commitment to our valued clients is to continue providing superior service by the friendliest folks in the real estate business. As always, we welcome your calls with real estate questions or concerns and your feedback (good and less good) is appreciated.

Free TV!
By special arrangement between ReMax International and EchoStar Communications, anyone who buys or sells a home through us—or any ReMax broker—by February 28, 2001, may receive free satellite installation and one month's free programming as a closing gift. If you plan to buy or sell anyway, this is an incentive to use ReMax. We're still waiting for details, but should have complete information on the program by March 15th.

Hot Water Heater Alert
Apparently all major brands of water heaters manufactured between 1993 and 1996 had an improperly formulated plastic "dip" tube that will degrade in the hot water of the tank. If your water heater was manufactured during that time or if you find small pieces of blue or green plastic in your tap screens or if your hot water supply runs out prematurely, your tank may be subject to a recall. For further details, go to http://mrfixit.net/featurearticles/features.htm or call 800-329-0561. Thanks to Paul MacGregor, Mr. Fixit on KNUS 710 for this info.

Mortgage News
Rates are up a bit from last month, but appear to be leveling off. Here's a sampling:
30-year fixed rate mortgage 8%
15-year fixed rate mortgage 7.25%

Adjustable rate mortgage 6.5%
The ARMs come in a variety of flavors, and their popularity has soared as rates have gone up. We're up 1.5% on average since a year ago.

Trivia
Who's going to the internet? 137 million people, still less than 50% of the nation's population. Average time spent per week is 8.2 hours. 11 million households are expected to make their first purchase online this year. Latin America will see the largest growth in web advertising this year: 137%. Online business-services revenues will climb to $43.7billion, almost double last year's $22 billion.

Tupper Briggs and The Mountain Home Team
RE/MAX Evergreen
30480 Stagecoach Blvd
Evergreen, CO 80439
(303) 670-6358 (direct)
(800) 568-6120 x40
(303) 670-9941 (fax)
tupper@tupperbriggs.com
www.tupperbriggs.com (Web site)

Be sure to visit our Web site. If you wish to be removed from this monthly update, please contact us.

E-Newsletter from Pat Zaby

Real Estate Focus by Pat Zaby, CRS, CRB, CCIM
July 25, 2000
http://www.patzaby.com

Does Your Web Site Make the Grade?

When agents are putting together a Web site, too many times they approach the project like they would to develop a personal brochure. The site ends up looking like personal promotion instead of providing a variety of meaningful services that customers will want.

When a customer comes onto our Web site, we should be entering their world, not forcing them to enter ours. It must be "you oriented" so that the customer feels like they are going to find what they're looking for in short order.

There are a lot of things that need to be considered and it is easy to leave out important items. Your personal Web site will be a constant work in progress and never be finished. If you can't manage the changes yourself, you'll need to budget for the maintenance.

If you don't constantly do research to find out what are the new, innovative features that can be offered, you'll need to hire someone who can do this for you. It can be an expensive project or an incredibly valuable investment that pays dividends in buyers and sellers many times over its cost.

The number one thing that buyers and sellers want when they go to a Web site is to see homes and as many pictures as possible. If you don't have a national consumer site attached to your Web site that lets them see not only your homes but everything else that is on the market, you aren't giving the public what they want.

Once the consumer has found a home that meets their needs, they want to be able to get additional information on the area, schools, and maps. Your site needs to have an integrated way to give them this information without them leaving your site.

The objective is to give them lots of information so that when they find something they want, they can use the "contact me" button that is on every page so that you can show it to them. The 1999 NAR Homebuying and Selling Survey has stated that people using the Internet are more likely to use a REALTOR® than those not using the Internet. They also buy a higher price home in a shorter period of time than those buyers not using the Internet.

Why wouldn't you create a strategy to work with more Internet buyers? You'll make more money, have more fun, and take control of your career.

Whether you currently have a Web site or you are researching what to do to start one, use the web site report card for evaluation. If yours doesn't make the grade, you'll know what you need to change it or what to look for from a new Web site developer.

Web Site Report Card

Multimedia
* Does it take longer than 8 seconds for your home page to load?
* Does it have a professional look and feel?
* Do you have a virtual tour? (IPIX, Bamboo, etc.)
* Does your site support audio and video?
* Do you have sound and a way to turn it off if the viewer doesn't want to hear it?

Marketing
* Do you list all of the services you provide?+
* Do you clearly state the areas that you work?+
* Do you state the benefits and advantages of doing business with you?
* Does your home page have your complete mailing address?+
* Does your home page have a complete ten digit phone number? Pager?
* Does your Web site have a complete name, phone number, and e-mail on every page?
* Is your site promoted to lots of search engines regularly?
* Do you have adequate meta-tags and keywords in your source?

Navigating
* Is there a link/button to return the viewer to the home page on every page?
* Does your site keep the customer on it rather than linking to another site?

Listings
* Are your personal listings available?
* Are you limited to how many listings you can show?
* Do you have a national listing database?
* How many multiple pictures are allowed for each listing?

* Does your site support a featured listing?
* Does your site support open houses?

Management
* Can you make changes to your site yourself?
* If yes, is there support to help you with the changes?
* If so, what hours are available?
* Can you upload listings yourself?
* Can you change the look and feel of your site at will?
* Does your site provide tracking tools?
* Do you sell positions on your site to offset the cost?

Convenience and Service
* Can a customer see your listings?+
* Can a customer see all listings available?
* Do you have mortgage calculators?
* Do you have interest rate quotes?
* Do you have local information links?
* Do you offer any special reports on specific home buying topics?
* Do you offer school information?
* Do you offer neighborhood information, including churches, shopping, etc.?
* Do you offer a link to maps?
* Do you offer a moving package, including change of address, driver's license, etc.?
* Do you offer real estate news?
* Do you have direct e-mail throughout the site?

Legal Issues
* Does every page in your Web site state that you are a real estate agent licensed in a particular state?*
* Does your company name appear wherever listing information is shown?*
* Does your state allow the agent name to be larger than the company name?
* Does it display a Fair Housing logo?
* Is your privacy policy posted? Is your agency disclosure posted?*

Grading Key (*10 points; +5 points; 2 points for every question)
90-100 A; 80-89 B; 70-79 C; 60-69 D; below 60 F

Through a special arrangement, you can get a personal Web site that will score an "A" on anyone's report card. You should consider looking at:
www.joanlohr.com <http://www.joanlohr.com>,
www.ggorman.com <http://www.ggorman.com>,
www.billbainbridge.com <http://www.billbainbridge.com>,
www.garyandnikkihomes.com
<http://www.garyandnikkihomes.com>, or
www.homes.com/mypersonalbrand
<http://www.homes.com/mypersonalbrand>.

The normal $495 set-up fee and the $70 domain registration fee will be waived if you act before August 15, 2000. The $199 basic training fee and the monthly hosting fee of $49 gets you your own personal domain name and a guarantee that any new developments that Homes.com offers will be included on your site. And if that isn't enough value for the money, included in the monthly fee you'll receive a complete version of the NEW PREP(tm) Suite 4.0, a $599 value.

Your e-Marketing solution is integrated in one package to work together to provide online and offline strategies that will increase your business. This opportunity is too good to pass up even if you currently have another Web site.

One additional bonus that you'll receive if you mention this newsletter when ordering your MyPersonalBrand Web site is the "Making It Make Sense" training CD ROM. This $99 value is a series of movies to show you how to get the most out of e-mail and your Internet browser by viewing movies on-screen that takes you through each step. It also includes the Real Estate Marketing Guide that has over 600 useful Web sites that are hyperlinked for convenience. This offer expires on August 1, 2000.

To receive this special pricing and the "Making It Make Sense" training CD bonus, call 972-991-1998 or contact sales@prepsoftware.com <mailto:sales@prepsoftware.com>.

Pat Zaby is a nationally known real estate speaker and trainer and vice president for Homes.com, Inc. He has a degree in real estate and holds four professional designations. He has been a REALTOR® since 1968, has been involved with automating real estate agents for over 14 years, and speaks to tens of thousands of people a year on the subject. For information about having Pat speak at your next event, contact seminars@patzaby.com <mailto:seminars@patzaby.com>.

Homes.com offers a successful Internet marketing strategy that includes your own permanent, personal domain name, the Homes.com Agent Advantage destination Web site, e-mail accounts, the New PREP(tm) Suite 4.0 with e-Marketing features, and training and coaching opportunities.

The NEW PREP Suite 4.0 includes e-Marketing features like direct email, mass email, email action plans, an Internet browser, totally re-designed content in presentations, postcards, notecards, flyers, and more. All four programs operate from one convenient window. You'll find the NEW PREP Suite 4.0 Easier...Faster...Better. PREP(tm) Software is a subsidiary of Homes.com, Inc.

Call today to adopt the Homes.com e-Marketing strategy. For information, phone 972-991-1998 or sales@prepsoftware.com or the Web site at http://www.prepsoftware.com.

Copyright Notice

Copyright 2000, Pat Zaby. All rights reserved. No part of this newsletter may be copied without written permission. Associations and companies may reproduce this newsletter in publications by contacting newsletter@patzaby.com.

If you wish to receive future email newsletters, subscribe to subscribe@patzaby.com. If you wish to be removed from future email newsletters, unsubscribe to unsubscribe@patzaby.com.

For general comments, questions or suggestions, please send an email to feedback@patzaby.com.

E-Newsletter from ePOWER!

```
                 e P O W E R!   N E W S
---------------------------------------------------------
Issue 4 / Volume 1  —  July 24, 2000
---------------------------------------------------------
"The Power Of People Connecting With People Through The
Internet"

A powerful resource for real estate professionals looking
tomaximize their online business with the Internet
EmpoweredConsumer™ (compliments of Mr. Internet!)

--------------------C O N T E N T S-------------------
* ePOWER! TIP: How To Check Your Site's Link Popularity
On Major Search Engines (simultaneously and for free!)...

* MAIN ARTICLE: How To Switch From AOL To The "Real"
Internet Without Losing Business

* e-PRO UPDATE: Now The World Knows About e-PRO! (The e-
PRO Consumer Awareness Site Is Live!)...

* SURVEY: How Well Do Agents Target Their Online
Markets?

* PARTING THOUGHTS: What Do You Stand For? -Converting
Lifelines To Taglines...
---------------------------------------------------------

** ePOWER! TIP: How To Check Your Site's Link Popularity
On Major Search Engines (simultaneously and for free!)...

Last month's survey was about how much "Link Popularity"
(I often refer to this as "Strategic Linking") agent
sites havein general. In that survey I gave a way to
quicklydetermine how many other sites link to yours
using the Altavista search engine.

Now I've found a much better way that will check
Altavista,Infoseek, Lycos, and AOL simultaneously.  It's
called LinkPopularity Check
(http://www.linkpopularitycheck.com), a free service from
the same search engine positioning experts that developed
Webposition Gold — the industry's pre-eminent search
engine positioning software.
```

This great service has some incredibly useful benefits:

a) You will know the competition! — You can compare your link popularity with up to 3 of your competitors at the same time (NOTE: it also indicates who is linking to them, a *very* important piece of intelligence if you want to quickly improve your site's link popularity);

b) You will save time. — Results are displayed graphically as well as numerically, so in one glance you can see where you stand against your competitors;

c) It can remind you to improve! — You can receive automatic link popularity results via e-mail every week if you want — a side benefit to this is that it is a constant reminder that improving your site's link popularity is an ongoing process.

This site also gives information on how to improve your site's link popularity index. However, after reviewing it I find it is not as focused as the article I wrote for REALTOR Magazine Online.
http://www.russer.com/~ami/981015/DMRI_98-10-15.html

Improving your "strategic linking" (a more focused and refined form of link popularity) is one of the most powerful and *sure* ways to drive highly qualified traffic to your site. And Link Popularity Check is the best tool I know of to measure your progress!

** MAIN ARTICLE: How To Switch From AOL To The "Real" Internet Without Losing Business

If you are currently suffering in A-O-Hell and want to switch to the "real" Internet, don't miss this article! It will take you step-by-step through how to migrate your online business from the training wheels of AOL to the full power that true Internet access and e-mail affords top Net-savvy real estate professionals.
http://www.russer.com/~ami/000615/dmri_00-06-15.html

(reprinted with permission from the August 2000 "Ask Mr. Internet!" REALTOR Magazine column)

** e-PRO UPDATE: Now The World Knows About e-PRO! (The e-PRO Consumer Awareness Site Is Live!)...

One of the things that makes the e-PRO certification unique from all other professional certifications / designations is that it is designed to be "Consumer Aware."

The newly launched e-PRO Consumer Awareness site is an important part of creating awareness (in the minds of the IEC™) as to the benefits of working with an e-PRO certified REALTOR. The site is called "THINK e-PRO!" and you can find it at http://www.thinkepro.com.

And this is just the beginning. Agents who become e-PRO certified also receive free marketing templates (which they can customize with their own brand) that detail the benefits of working with an online real estate professional. Later this year, look for national press coverage too, as the word of e-PRO reaches the masses in a big way.

Remember, the Internet Empowered Consumer will *always* get what they want. And they want real estate professionals that know how to work with them effectively — on *their* terms. Set yourself apart in the eyes of your online consumers. If you are not already registered don't wait — Go e-PRO! You can sign up right now at http://www.eproinfo.com.

** SURVEY: How Well Do Agents Target Their Online Markets?

##
WIN A COPY OF ePOWER! — the "bible" of doing business on the Net for real estate professionals (a $99 value) just by completing this survey!

LAST MONTH'S WINNER — Larry Daniel (an e-PRO 500 graduate and pioneer Internet REALTOR extraordinaire!) of Keller Williams Realty in Springfield, MO. (http://www.OzarksHome.com) He was the first to identify Ghandi.net as the domain name registrar (http://www.ghandi.net) offering the lowest price for a 1 year registration — $12 Euros or about $11 US. Great job Larry and special thanks from Mr. Internet for being a player!

##

Lack of target marketing is one of the primary reasons most agents don't even come close to reaching their potential online. This survey is designed to give us an idea of the range of targeting that is be done and share the clever ideas that some people use to fine tune their targeting efforts. To view the survey, just go to http://www.zoomerang.com/survey.zgi?W3C935LPHPHFS9TQVYKG1G4H

To view the eye-opening results of last month's survey ("How Well Are You 'Strategically Linked'?") just go to http://www.russer.com/surveys/epower_news/ri4v1/r_000701.htm

----

** PARTING THOUGHTS: What Do You Stand For? —Converting Lifelines To Taglines...

What do you stand for? Aside from raising a family, making money, and building a successful career, is there something bigger than you that you are passionate about?

Someone (I forget who...) once said that extraordinary people are just ordinary individuals who have chosen to commit to extraordinary acts or ways of "being" (my paraphrase). It seems that many "great" people were those that took a stand for something that was simple yet huge and the results they achieved reflected it. Dr. Martin Luther King, Ghandi, and Mother Teresa are all examples of ordinary people being extraordinary as a result of their "stand."

However, you don't have to be a martyr or a saint to take a stand in your business. It does mean, however, being passionate about something bigger than you — which typically means your customers, in some unique way or context.

For example, from day one, I have stood for "all people empowered by the Internet." This stand comes from my deep belief that the Internet is the most important thing to connect humanity since religion. I "declare" this stand on every page of my Web site and with every e-mail via my "tag-line": "The Power Of People Connecting With People Through The Internet."

Michel Fortin, a highly respected international Internet marketing consultant (http://www.michelfortin.com) has "Turning Businesses Into Powerful Magnets" as his tag-line. Can you guess what he stands for?

When I speak to thousands of agents around the country I urge them to create tag-lines for each of their online target markets. However, it is tough to come up with a convincing, effective tag-line if you really are not clear about what you stand for. The best, most powerful tag-lines are based on an individual's "life-lines" — which are just those things you are clearly passionate about that happen to be bigger than, and outside of, you.

Take a moment (or two) to think about what you really stand for. Then take those life-lines and turn them into to powerful tag-lines that you proudly shout to the whole world, and watch your online business become extraordinary!

Have great Net Success!

~ Mr. Internet ~

------------------P O S T   S C R I P T-----------------

If you find this information valuable, please forward it on to a friend!

Your suggestions and comments are welcome! Send them to mailto:suggestions@epowernews.com.

To visit Mr. Internet's Web site, just go to http://www.russer.com.

For permission to reprint this or any article from ePOWER NEWS, please contact Renea Solis at mailto:rsolis@russer.com.

```
------------------------------------------------------------
You are currently subscribed to epower_news as:
terri@terrimurphy.com.

To unsubscribe, send a blank email to mailto:leave-
epower_news-1526921Y@lists.epowernews.com

To subscribe, send a blank email to mailto:join-
epower_news@lists.epowernews.com
------------------------------------------------------------

ePOWER™, Mr. Internet™, Internet Empowered Consumer™,
IEC™, and Rules Of Engagement™, are all trademarks of
RUSSER Communications
------------------------------------------------------------

ISSN: 1530-5252 - Library Of Congress, Washington D.C.,
USA. Copyright © 2000 RUSSER Communications, all rights
reserved. You may forward this newsletter only in its
entirety including this copyright notice.
```

E-Newsletter from Allen F. Hainge Seminars

```
REAL ESTATE TECHNOLOGY NEWS & VIEWS
On-Line Edition, July 24, 2000
A Free On-Line Real Estate Technology Newsletter From
Allen F. Hainge, CRS, Allen F. Hainge Seminars, Inc.
Web Site: http://www.afhseminars.com
Email: news@afhseminars.com

CONTENTS:
* Email On The Road
* EPA Info On The Web
* Know The Neighborhood & Autoresponders
* Seattle CyberStar(tm) National Tour Seminar
* If You Change Email Addresses
* Back To The Basics: Reducing Photo Size For Emailing
* CyberStar(tm) Tip Of The Week: WinFax Pro

============================================================
Real Estate Technology News & Views is sponsored by the
Web site choice of today's top real estate
professionals, MyPersonalBrand.Com. Provided by
Homes.com, MyPersonalBrand.com is an inexpensive,
content-rich and effective solution to generating Web
```

business! Find out more about MyPersonalBrand.Com's turnkey Web marketing solution at http://www.mypersonalbrand.com.

EMAIL ON THE ROAD

It's vacation time again (I'm in Hawaii at present), and if you have a notebook computer with you on vacation, there's no need to let the email pile up awaiting your return. Allen F. Hainge CyberStar(tm) Arleen Yobs of Roy Wheeler Realty Company in Charlottesville, VA (http://www.arleenyobs.com) passes along this suggestion about some "traveling" email services she uses:

"I'm at the Outer Banks with my 18 year old son and his high school graduating buddies. I am emailing from http://www.freewwweb.com with a local Internet dial up to my webmail.intelos.com site. Also fairly pleased with www.ureach.com, the service that Linda Soesbe mentioned to us CyberStars(tm) a while back. The voicemail program is great and you get 60 free minutes the first month (great for summer vacation time!) and 30 free minutes each month thereafter!

EPA INFO ON THE WEB

You can see a list of EPA regulated facilities by zip code at http://www.epa.gov/epahome/comm.htm. You can get a report on each facility or problem area mentioned and can even see a map pinpointing potential problem areas. This could come in handy in order to avoid selling properties that might be near areas of concern to purchasers. Lots of other useful information on the site, http://www.epa.gov.

KNOW THE NEIGHBORHOOD & AUTORESPONDERS

CyberStar(tm) Teri Isner of Main Street Realtors, Orlando, FL (http://www.teriisner.com) is combining an auto responder on her Web site and Know The Neighborhood (eNeighborhood) reports to increase her site's effectiveness.

As you probably know, an auto responder is an application your site designer installs on your site so that whenever someone clicks on a link, they automatically receive something right away via email. Lots of uses for auto responders, chief among them is the fact that they make it possible for someone sending an inquiry to get an immediate response, even if you're away from your computer. Teri and her Web designer, Sandy Teller of Internet Online Programs (http://www.programs.com), have made it possible for anyone requesting specific neighborhood information for a property to get a very thorough, great looking report right away. Teri "prints" her eNeighborhood reports using HotSend (http://www.hotsend.com), which automatically saves it as a file. She sends the file to Sandy, who sets up an auto responder. People receive the KTN info as an .exe file by e-mail.

Teri only has to save the file once using HotSend. She doesn't have to mess with mailing it out, she saves money on postage, and she gets the email address for follow up for any person requesting the info.

If you're going to ask your Web designer to institute this idea, ask him or her if the auto responders used at your site will send "binary" attachments, the form used by the eNeighborhood reports. Also, be aware that the file itself, if you do a 12 page report, is about 420K, so you might put a "this will take a couple of minutes to download" notice by the link.

(eNeighborhoods is an Allen F. Hainge CyberStar(tm) recommended product. For information on our discount price or to order, contact Dixie Murphy at dixie@afhseminars.com or call her at 800-695-3794. eNeighborhood carries our 30 day money back guarantee: you don't like it, send it back for a full refund!)

SEATTLE CYBERSTAR(tm) NATIONAL TOUR SEMINAR

"Finally, a seminar that gives you the inside 'how to' and doesn't just sell you products!" This was among the comments from Paul O'Connell of Coldwell Banker At Your Service Realty in Rochester, MN, after he attended our

in CyberStar(tm) National Tour Seminar in Minneapolis. You, too, will have great comments after attending our upcoming seminar in Seattle on Thursday, September 14th, at the Radisson Hotel Seattle Airport.

Sales associate panelists Niel Thomas of Coldwell Banker Fortune, Anchorage, AK (http://www.nielt.com), Roger Lautt of RE/MAX Exclusive Properties, Chicago, IL (http://www.isellchicago.com) and Doug Whitehouse of Hannett, Wilson, & Whitehouse LLC Realtors, Bloomfield Hills, MI (http://www.whitehouses.com) will spend all day sharing with you *specifically* what technology works for them in today's market: how to have a Web site that earns from $20,000-$300,000 a year, how to market using digital cameras, Web marketing strategies, online and on your Web site newsletters that work, marketing with multimedia presentations, effective printed presentations...and much, much more. For a full description of the seminar content, go to http://www.afhseminars.com/tourinfo.htm.

Not sure it's for you? Here's what attendee Jean Luedde of Valledor Company Realtors, Miami, FL, had to say after the seminar she attended: "Where else in the world of real estate seminars can you get this amount of profit-making ideas for so little money? This should be a 'must attend' for every agent, whether you've been in the business for 6 months or 25 years!"

We've had attendees back for their 2nd and even 3rd CyberStar(tm) National Tour Seminar....come see why! Be sure to click on the "testimonials" link to see what others say about their experience. NOTE: The CyberStar(tm) National Tour Seminars are presented in Plain English, not Techie Talk! EACH PANELIST IS A PRACTICING SALES ASSOCIATE, JUST LIKE YOU! They're not paid to be there: they come because they want to share with you in simple terms how you can achieve greater success in your marketplace!

The all day seminar is sponsored by the Washington State CRS Chapter and carries 7.5 Washington State clock hours C.E. The price is $129, which includes a CyberStar(tm) Networking Luncheon, but you can sign up for just $99 if you register by September 7th. To register, either call my assistant, Dixie Murphy, at 800-695-3794, email her

at dixie@afhseminars.com, or register online at
http://www.afhseminars.com/tourinfo.htm.

IF YOU CHANGE EMAIL ADDRESSES

If you change email addresses (you switch from AOL to an ISP, for example), be sure to let us know of the switch via email if you want to continue receiving our newsletter. When I send out an issue from our list serve, we always get a number of "non-deliverable" email addresses in response to the mailing. Consequently, the addresses are automatically removed from our mailing list. So, if you switch, email Dixie at dixie@afhseminars.com to continue receiving your newsletter.

BACK TO THE BASICS: REDUCING PHOTO SIZE FOR EMAILING

Emailing photos as attachments to your emails can really increase your income. Just a few of the uses: email photos of other homes you have listed to those who visit your open houses, email a photo of the seller's home to the seller prior to your listing presentation, email construction photos to those out-of-towners who buy new construction from you, etc.

One problem I see with many sales associates who email photos, however, is that they email *large* photos, photos that take a long time to download. Emailing such photos can cause irritation rather than provide a service. So, here are a few tips on making sure that the photos you use are small enough to download quickly:

* Set your camera for the lowest resolution if you know you're going to email the photo you're taking.

* Bring the photo from your camera into a photo imaging software that's on your computer. I use the photo imaging software that comes with PictureWorks, but you probably have access to another program if you don't use PictureWorks: Microsoft PhotoEditor, the software you installed when you got your digital camera, Adobe PhotoShop, etc.

* Get the exact photo you want by cropping the original, changing the contrast, eliminating the garbage can in front of the house, etc.

* REDUCE THE PHOTO'S SIZE. While on vacation here on the Big Island in Hawaii, for example, I took a photo using the medium resolution setting on my Kodak DC260, since I may want to make a print of the photo later and would want the better quality for the print. I brought up the original photo, which was 201K in size. (I could email this, but it would be a large file. I know that by resizing the photo, I can get the same quality for emailing but in a much smaller size.) into HotShots (part of PictureWorks) and clicked on Image/Resize. This showed me the dimensions of the original photo, 1760x1168 pixels, in a small window. I changed the first number to 500. Since "Preserve Aspect Ratio" was checked, the second number automatically changed. The measurements now read 500x332 pixels. (BTW: I'm no expert on "pixels": I just know that if I reduce those numbers, I get a smaller photo for emailing!). I then clicked OK for the new measurements to take effect. IMPORTANT: I then clicked File/Save As (not File/Save) to save the picture. This means that I'll be saving the smaller copy of the picture and the original will be saved just as it was, since it won't be overwritten, as it would if I clicked File/Save. PictureWorks then asked me to choose a directory in which to save the smaller photo and to give it a name. I did so, then clicked Save. HotShots then shows me a bar labeled "Quality." I chose 50%, which further reduced the photo's size, then continued saving the photo.

The result? The original photo of 201K became a smaller photo of only 22K, a perfect size for quick uploading and downloading. Remember: since I used File/Save As, I still have the original photo for use later on if I want it.

So...learn how to resize your photos using your photo imaging software. If it all looks confusing to you, get the techie in for a quick lesson: once you work through it, you'll easily be able to do it next time, and the recipients of your photos won't be cursing your name as they wait for large files to download!

CYBERSTAR(tm) TIP OF THE WEEK: WINFAX PRO SOFTWARE

This week's tip comes from Allen F. Hainge CyberStar(tm) Tim M. Kinzler, CRS, of Arvida Realty Services, Delray Beach, FL (http://www.timkinzler.com). Tim, you'll remember, is the one who takes his digital camera to all Realtor meetings and conventions, takes a bunch of photos, then emails them to folks he met during the meetings, thus building up his referral base. Here's Tim's take on WinFax Pro
(http://www.symantec.com/winfax/index.html).

"One product I really recommend is WinfaxPro software. Using it, you can send/receive faxes right from your computer. Its many features include drag and drop faxing, broadcast faxing, integration with Microsoft Outlook, "junk" fax management, and more.

"As an example of how I use the program, I leave my computer on and leave the fax software open. Any fax sent to me gets saved in my computer. I can have the computer then:

* Print the fax for my review
* Forward the fax to a number where I want it to go, including to a hotel while I'm out-of-town
* Forward a fax to a group, which could include all parties to a transaction
* Make notes on the fax without printing it, then return it to the sender

"When doing contracts with contract software, I can send via fax as well as email without printing, thus maintaining the quality of document and avoiding fax papers getting tangled in sending the fax!"

Copyright 2000 by Allen F. Hainge Seminars, Inc. All rights reserved. No part of this material may be used or reproduced for commercial gain or stored in a database or retrieval system without prior written permission of the publisher, except in the case of brief quotations embodied in critical articles or reviews. Email comments, subscription or unsubscribe requests to news@afhseminars.com.

<<<>>> <<<>>> <<<>>> <<<>>> <<<>>> <<<>>> <<<>>> <<<>>>
* To remove yourself from this mailing list, point your browser to:
http://www.postmastergeneral.com/remove?allenhainge
* Enter your email address (terri@terrimurphy.com) in the field provided and click "Unsubscribe". The mailing list ID is "allenhainge".

OR...

* Reply to this message with the word "remove" in the subject line.

This message was sent to address terri@terrimurphy.com
X-PMG-Recipient: terri@terrimurphy.com
<<<>>> <<<>>> <<<>>> <<<>>> <<<>>> <<<>>> <<<>>> <<<>>>

Index

A

ACT, 10
Advertising, including e-mail address in, 92
Agent2000, 10, 121, 162
Ancillary services, 18
  in listing presentations, 158
  in prelisting package, 118-19
AOL, 36, 38, 81
Armitage, Diane, 174-75
AT&T, 38
Automation Quest Programs, 169-70
Auto responders, 24, 63-66
  benefits of, 66, 163
  in e-newsletters, 69
  fees for, 65-66
  getting, 65-66

B

Back-end services, 22-23, 164
Backing up data, 57, 199-203
Bailey, Joseph, 183
Baker, Tim, 97-98

Big Rock Theory, 181
Blue Mountain Greeting Cards, 17-18
Bookkeeping, 9-10
Branding, 46, 73, 86
Breathnach, Sarah Ban, 183
Brinton, Howard, Seminars, 6
Browser software, 50
Bulletin board, 73-74
Business information center, 74
Business plan, 109, 168
  developing, 12-14, 195
Business providers, 37-39, 46, 81
Buyer assistant, working as, 5
Buyers. *See also* Real estate clients; Real estate customers
  information on average, 158
  matching, with real estate agents, 30-31

C

Cable modem, 82
Call-in, 22
Carlson, Richard, 183
Case sensitivity, 47, 90

Chill out day, 183
Clean Kids Club membership form, 125-26
Coaching, 168-69
Companion services, linking to, 86
Competitive pricing, 25
CompuServe, 81
Concierge style service team, 21-22, 118-19
ConsumerReportsOnline®, 25
Consumers in driving real estate industry, 17-20
Content, linking for, 84-86
Content providers, 37-39, 81
Contractor repairs, 18
Covey, Stephen, 181
Customer services, providing, 23-25

D

Data, backing up, 57, 199-203
Databases, digital, 10-11, 98, 196-97
Data mining, 59, 87
Date night, 182
Delegating, 186
Deleting, 186
Desktop, 50
Digital communication, 27-48
  prospecting in, 30-31
  understanding service requirements in, 27-30
Digital databases, 10-11, 98, 196-97
Digital listening presentation, 128
Digital Subscriber Line (DSL) connectivity, 82
Discount opportunities, 18, 87
Distribution lists, building, 59-61
Domain, 33-35
  benefits of having own, 36, 73
  choosing, 79
  need for own, 78-79
  registering, 34-35, 40, 79-80

E

Earthlink, 37, 8

*e*KEY, 164-65, 173
Electronic folders
  creating, 55-56
  uses for, 56-57
Electronic key boxes, 164-65
e-mail addresses
  capturing, 58-59
  printing on business cards, 89
  unlimited capability, 83
e-mail communications, 23-24, 32
  attachments in, 37
  auto responders for, 24, 63-66, 69, 163
  checking for messages, 107
  connection in, 32-33
  correct spelling and punctuation in, 44-45
  defining expectations for, in prelisting package, 121-23
  demonstrating power of tools, 163
  domain in, 33-35
    benefits of having own, 36, 73
    choosing, 79
    need for own, 78-79
    registering, 34-35, 40, 79-80
  emoticons in, 43
  finding hosting service, 35-36
  as form of farming, 96
  forwarding of, 83
  getting permanent address for, 45-46
  making it work, 41-45, 47-48
  "netiquette" in, 42-45, 46
  passwords in, 39-41, 47
  registering domain in, 34-35
  selecting Internet Service Provider, 36-41
  user names in, 39-41
  Web-based, 62-63
e-mail managers, 49-62
  automation and, 51-55
  backing up data, 57
  benefits of using, 49-51
  building distribution lists, 59-61
  in capturing e-mail addresses, 58-59

electronic folders in
 creation of, 55-56
 uses for, 56-57
e-mail signatures, 43-44, 46-47
 auto responder in, 64-65
 making automatic, 52-55
 multipurposed, 54
Emoticons, 43
Encryption, 37
e-newsletters, 47, 61-62
 auto responder in, 69
 benefits of, 105-6
 demonstrating power of, 163
 for farming, 106-7
 getting sponsor for, 69
 including Frequently Asked
   Questions in, 69
 length of, 107
 making blank template for, 68
 naming, 68
 requesting comments from readers, 68-69
 sample, 205-25
 subjects for, 68
 uses of, 101-2
E-POWER: Online Success Strategies for Real Estate Professionals, 170
e-Pro, 170-71
Eudora™, 50
Exit strategy, developing and planning, 196-97

F

Family nights, 182-83
Farming, 61, 95-107
 in building prospects, 106
 e-mail as, 96, 98
 e-newsletters in, 106-7
 mail lists in, 100-101
 maximizing theme in, 97-98
 techniques in, 61-62
 tools for, 99-106

File Transfer Protocol, unlimited access to, 83
Fitness, taking time for, 184
Flaming, 103-4
Follow-up system, 22-23
Forgiving, 187-88
Framing, 24. *See also* Linking
Frequently Asked Questions (FAQs), including, in e-newsletters, 69

G

Gateway, 16
Gegax, Tom, 168
Gerber, Michael, 8-9, 13
Global, 37, 81
Goals, planning your, 196
Goldmine, 10
Gratitude, 189-90
Great service sites, 24-25
GTE, 37, 81

H

Hainge, Allen, Seminars and Newsletters, 6, 172
Hardware, investing in, 11-12
Hoffmann, Barbara, 170
HomeAdvisor™, 17
HomeBid.com, 24
HomeGain.com, 20, 24-25, 30-31
Home page, 73
 having on company's Web site, 77
Homes.com, 22-23, 106
HomeSeekers™, 17
HomeSeekers.com, 76
Homesellers. *See also* Real estate clients; Real estate customers
 matching, with real estate agents, 30-31
Hosting service, 80-83
 finding, 35-36, 40-41

I

Improvenet.com, 24

The Industry Standard, 172
Information, links for, 171
Informational reports and updates, 24
Informational services for customers, 87
Inman, 16
Inman News, 172
InmanNews.com, 25
Inspections, 18
Instant messaging, 23, 63–66
Internet Explorer, 50–51
Internet marketing strategy, 129–130
Internet Service Provider (ISP), 32–33, 35, 80–83
  business providers, 37–39, 46, 81
  content providers, 37–39, 81
  mail list software offered by, 10
  selecting, 36–41, 82
Internet showcase, 74
Interview with successful real estate agent, 5–7
iSucceed™.com, 6, 25

K

Kiosks, 63
Knox, David, 126–27

L

Laptop computers, 159
Lead, 22
Letter of introduction for prelisting package, 112–13
Life balance, 177–97
Linking, 24, 76, 84–86
  to companion services, 86
  for content, 84–86
  to great service sites, 24–25
  for training and information, 171
Listing interviews, using presentation software for, 159
Listing presentation, 157–66
  client expectations in, 157
  components of, 160–65
  customizing, with tech tools, 160
  demonstrating power of electronic communication tools, 163
  demonstrating power of e-newsletters, 163
  demonstrating samples of special reports, 162
  digital technology in, 128, 158–60
  electronic key boxes in, 164–65
  featuring personal Web presence in, 161
  featuring special services and statistics on company, 161
  getting seller's commitment for, 120–21
  including information on Web sites where home will be featured, 161
  keeping seller connected in, 164
  offering information on latest sites in, 164
  showing off site tracking capabilities, 162
  software for, 159
  taking seller on virtual tour in, 163–64
ListServs. *See* Mail lists
Lurking, 103
Lycos.com, 90–91

M

Mail lists, 67–69
  benefits of, 105–6
  contributing to, 103
  coolness on, 103–5
  in farming, 100–101
  header for, 101–2
  one-way, 67, 102
  other uses for, 101–2
  posting to, 104
  replying to, 104
  software for, 10
  tips on writing to, 68–69
  two-way, 67, 103
  types of, 102–3

Marketing plan, defining, 196
Mentor, finding, 3-5, 13
Microsoft.com, 76
Microsoft Internet Explorer, 50-51
Microsoft PowerPoint, 159
Mindspring, 37
Mitchell, W., 189

N

National Association of Realtors®, 170
"Netiquette," 42-45, 46
Netscape, 16, 50, 51
Newton, Jim, 183

O

Objectives, planning your, 196
One-way mail list, 67, 102
Outlook, 50
Outlook Express, 50

P

Paranych, Terry, 124
Passwords, 39-41, 65
　as case sensitive, 47, 90
Personal assistant, 5
Personal Digital Assistant (PDA), 172-74
Personal mission statement in prelisting package, 114
Portal, 16
Prelisting package, 109-55
　for advanced agents, 127-28
　ancillary service team in, 118-19
　Clean Kids Club membership form, 125-26
　creativity in, 128
　defining business strategies and policies in, 119-20
　defining expectations for communication, 121-23
　delivery of, 111-12
　getting seller's commitment on home presentation in, 120-21
　homework in, 115-16
　information content in, 123-24
　letter of introduction in, 112-13
　objective of, 110-11
　organization of, 113-25
　personal mission statement, 114
　questionnaire, 116-17
　sample, 124-25, 131-55
　selling team in, 117-18
　showing off Web presence in, 114-15
　table of contents in, 124
　video training and information tapes, 126-28
　virtual tours in, 124
Prepura, Wayne, 182
Presentation. *See* Listing presentation
Presentation software, learning to use for listing interviews, 159
Pricing, competitive, 25
Print media, 45, 47
Prodigy, 36, 81
Productivity software, 22-23, 192
Professional, consulting a, 195
Prospecting, 30-31
　e-farming in, 106
Punctuation, 44-45

Q

Questionnaire, in prelisting package, 116-17
QuickBooks©, 9
Quicken©, 9

R

Read/write CDs, 201, 202
Real estate, investing in, 197
Real estate agents
　benefits provided by, 20-22
　interviewing successful, 5-7
　locating on Internet, 88-90
　matching homesellers and buyers with, 30-31
　need for business plan, 12-14

prelisting packages for advanced, 127-28
selecting, 20-23
service ratios of, 4-5
success model for, 4-5
working as buyer assistant under, 5
working as licensed personal assistant under, 5
Real estate business
  creating digital database for, 10-11
  developing business plan for, 12-14
  finding mentor in, 3-5, 13
  getting a technology coach in, 11
  getting training in, 12
  investing in hardware and software, 11-12
  keeping good records in, 8-10
  treating as real business, 7-8
Real estate clients
  expectations of, 157
  locating agents on Internet by, 88-90
Real estate customers, 17-20
  changes in, 1-2
  information services for, 87
  matching with agents, 30-31
  providing services to, 23-25, 158-59
  service requirements of digital, 27-30
Real Estate Data, 172
Real estate industry
  changes in, 2-3, 14
  consumers in driving, 17-20
  new challenges for services in, 17
Reality, 188-89
Realtor.com™, 17, 42, 76
Realty Times, 172
RealtyTimes.com, 25
Records, keeping good, 8-10
Refocusing, 178-81
Relationships, building, 192-93
Resource books, 175-76
Résumé page, 16
Russer, Michael, 170

S

Screen captures, 160
Search engines, 90-91
Security, planning, 193-97
Seller. *See also* Real estate clients; Real estate customers
  getting commitment for home presentation from, 120-21
Service ratios, 4
Services, new challenges for, 17
Shead, Jim, 89
Software
  bookkeeping, 9-10
  browser, 50
  investing in, 11-12
  mail list, 10
  for Palm Pilot, 173
  presentation, 159
  productivity, 22-23, 192
  site tracking, 88
  tracking, 194
Spamming, 100, 107
Specific events, planning for, 182
Specific profile information, 74
Spelling, 44-45
Sprint, 38, 81
Star Power© tapes, 6
Superdisk, 201, 202
SUPRA® eKEY, 164-65, 173

T

Tape, 202
Technology coach, 11
Tech tools, customizing presentation with, 160
Time management, 9-10, 185-86
Tite, 18
Top Presenter®, 159
TopProducer™, 10, 121, 122, 162
  Contact manager software, 173
Tracking software, 194
Tracking system, 22-23
Training, 18
  links for, 171

need for, 12
video, 126-28
Trump, Donald, 177-78
Tuccillo, John, 21, 60
Two-way mail list, 67, 103

U

Unlimited File Transfer Protocol access, 83
URL (Universal Resource Locator), 15, 33, 34, 78-83
User names, 39-41

V

Vacation days, 184
Value-set parameters, 4
Video training and informational tapes, 126-28
Virtual assistant, 74
Virtual tour, taking seller on, 124, 163-64
Voice mail, including e-mail address in, 92

W

Web address, 78-83
  printing on business cards, 89
Web-based e-mail, 62-63
Webcrawler.com, 90-91
Web marketing, personal promotion strategy in, 88-91
Web presence, 71-93
  expectations of, 72-73
  featuring personal, 161
  showing off, 114-15
Web sites
  announcing, 92
  back-end services offered by, 22-23
  bulletin board as, 73-74
  content-intensive, 93
  directing traffic to, 91-93

discounted services on, 17
ease of use, 19
expectations of, 72-73
featuring of homes in, 161
having home page on company's, 77
home pages at, 73
hot links to great, 24-25
immediacy of, 19
indexing, 90
keys to effective planning of, 75-77
linking
  to companion services, 86
  for content, 84-86
  to great service, 24-25
  with other sources, 76
making changes to, 83
options on, 19-20
portals as, 16
résumé page as, 16
style of, 84
tracking, 88
  showing off, 162
types of, 73-74
uses of, 74
Web site services, 24
Websuite.com, 22-23, 106, 170
World Wide Web, defined, 15-17

X

XML (eXtensible Markup Language), 91

Y

Yahoo, 90

Z

Zaby, Pat, 121
ZDNet, 16
Zip disk, 201-2

About the Author

Terri Murphy, GRI, CRS, and LTG, is an active REALTOR® licensed in Illinois for over 21 years. For most of those years she rose to the top of her profession by listing and selling over 100 properties a year consistently with a never ending quest for learning how to work smarter and not harder. Dearborn published her first book in 1996, *Terri Murphy's Listing & Selling Secrets: How to Become a Million Dollar Producer.* She is a staff writer for several publications, including *Real Estate Professional.*

Terri consults with many of the major forces in the real estate industry. Most recently she has been instrumental in the development of content and as a spokesperson and speaker for *iSucceed.com,* a revolutionary on-line training and education portal. Audiences across the country enjoy her friendly style, panache, and humor as she delivers a high energy/high content program to give agents a game plan to maximize the advantages of the Internet in doing business today.